A Legacy Undone

... AN EXTRAORDINARY TRUE LIFE
EXPERIENCE THAT WILL MAKE YOU
RETHINK PROTECTING YOUR FAMILY

TERRIE & JON HULL

Clovercroft Publishing

A Legacy Undone: An Extraordinary True Life Experience
That Will Make You Rethink Protecting Your Family

©2015 by Jon and Terrie Hull

Published by Clovercroft Publishing, Franklin, Tennessee

Cover Design by Debbie Manning Sheppard

Interior Design by Suzanne Lawing

Editing by Tammy Kling

Printed in the United States of America

978-1-940262-95-6

This book is dedicated to all of you ~ the fathers and mothers, sons and daughters ~ who plan and strive to be good stewards of their families, no matter what.

"Prepare for the unknown by studying how others in the past have coped with the unforeseeable and the unpredictable."

—GEORGE S. PATTON

What's Your Legacy?

We ask this question because your legacy is something to plan for, and to intentionally care about. If you have a family, it's possible you've already planned for your will, estate documents, and maybe even medical wishes, but have you considered everything?

Are you prepared for the unexpected?

We wanted to write this book for a myriad of reasons, and in some ways, we had to write it to express the thick feelings of sadness, despair, anxiety, and anger we had experienced over the sudden and unexpected events in our family.

Years ago, when we were faced with this unexpected situation in our lives, we felt like we had lost so much. But looking back, we can see how we really were prepared in many ways and unprepared in others. Whether you're facing an illness or death in the family, an aging parent, or proactively planning for the future, we are here for you by providing the resources you will need to prepare for that event.

We are committed to working with life planning agencies, estate planning attorneys, legal organizations, and healthcare professionals to help educate and bring awareness to individuals about the contingencies of life, protecting your family and your assets. We've learned that there is a lot of misinformation out there, and the majority of people are uninformed. As we wrote this book we felt that this story touched on many life experiences which people could relate to and/or learn from. Even the most loving families can be separated by unexpected circumstances and the undue influences of others.

One of the things most people don't understand is how quickly and drastically life events can change our lives. Most don't realize how vulnerable the elderly can be and how an unexpected incident, like a car crash or an injury, can drastically alter your life forever. It is important to have the legal necessities in place for your family because it will make the difference between protecting your assets or losing everything you've worked and hoped for. In our case we lost a loving mother because she was isolated and then separated from the family.

Our message? Don't wait.

Put your affairs in order starting today. For some families, this conversation has become lost or never started. For others, there are the myths that this is about death and only elderly people have this concern. Our story will show you how putting your affairs in order is about life, love, family, security, financial savvy, and the legal system. It is one of the most critical and caring family decisions you can make. It is one of the best ways to secure everything you have worked so hard for and to legally secure your rights, assets, legacy, and wishes. It is also one of the most important things to teach your children as they move into adulthood.

You might be surprised to learn that the birth of the information age created a new legal danger for families—Internet passwords for social networks, business websites, and financial and personal interest sites. Have you legally assigned a loved one to hold power of attorney for your passwords? If not, that loved one will be burdened with a mostly unknown part of the legal system that will result in even more grief for them should something happen to you.

Take Facebook for example. Did you know that the user name and password are part of a binding agreement as part of their terms of use agreement? Did you know that if something happened to you and you had not shared your login information with someone close to you, nobody could access your Facebook page. When that happens, Facebook will not release the login information with anybody, not a spouse, child, mother, or father.

Once someone dies, you may no longer have access to that account, and the service provider is legally allowed to delete the account, but will not give you access to that account unless you have the legal authority to access it. Passwords are considered part of a separate, independent contract with each provider. The terms of use are that you agree to maintain that you are the sole provider, with login credentials, to get into your sites. Yet most people believe their kids and grandchildren will be able to access their Facebook site after they die and see all the memories and photos there. That's not true—unless you plan for it.

Here is our story; hold on tight . . .

CHAPTER 1

Terrie's Story

I first began to realize something was wrong the day I met Mom and her new caregiver at the occupational therapist's office. Mom seemed really distant that day.

She was never at ease during these appointments because the occupational therapist would ask her all kinds of questions that she'd have to think really hard to answer. She would always ask Mom to draw a clock, which Mom could never do; but on this visit, when the caregiver started coming in, Mom seemed especially nervous.

I told the caregiver that she could stay in the waiting room, but she insisted that Mom wanted her to come in. When I asked why, the caregiver told me that my mother wanted her to take notes, which I didn't understand at all. It was very confusing.

My mother had been a vibrant woman all of her life, so seeing her this way was unreal. She had always been happy, bubbly, and joyous and always had a song for everything. A career elementary school music teacher who loved to sing, mom had always been very involved with the Oregon Association of Educators and had even sat on the board. I admired her strength and independence. She was active in her church and volunteered every week, lending a helping hand whenever it was needed. She was funny, and intelligent, and far more than just my mother! My Mom was one of my best friends.

But then things started to shift. I had heard stories about people with loving mothers who suddenly changed when diseases such as Alzheimer's or some other form of dementia set in, but I never imagined I'd experience it myself. When you think of your parents, you think of your protectors, your teachers, those who will be there for you, and vice versa. As a child, I don't think it ever occurs to you how quickly things can change. But when my father died, things did change. My mother changed.

She became introverted and lonely, so I tried to comfort her. We would spend long hours on the phone every night, and talked about life and things that would give her hope for the future. I began to see a light at the end of the tunnel as she started to get back to her ordinary self.

My mother began taking dance lessons, and at one lesson, she met Billy, a man who seemed to reignite her passion for life. I was overjoyed to see Mom happy again!

I was so focused on her happiness that I suppose I didn't see the red flags on the road ahead. I didn't see the warning signs along the way until it was too late. Looking back I must admit that my husband Jon had reservations about Billy from the start. Although we knew very little about him, you know when you just feel a bad energy about someone, and Billy had bad energy about him. A man well into his seventies, his hair gray and a stature that showed a body in decline. Although an average-looking fellow, he was a smooth talker. But he seemed decidedly disinterested in us.

In March, 2011, I received a call that my mom had been involved in a serious car wreck on the interstate. Investigations would show that she had been rear-ended by a man traveling 45 miles per hour faster than her, and the impact had sent her vehicle flying into the meridian, where she struck a concrete barricade. Her car was totaled. Mom struck her head twice in the impact, once on the back left from the initial impact, and then again on her upper forehead when she hit the barricade. I immediately panicked when I heard the news. I called my husband right away.

JON'S STORY

I got the call late in the afternoon.

I was still at my office, and Terrie was frantic as she explained that her mother was involved in a car accident on the interstate not far from our home. The first responders had taken her unconscious to an emergency room, but needed to move her to a hospital that had better facilities for the head injuries she had suffered. Terrie seemed as if she was handling the situation well. She knew her mother's insurance company information and was quickly able to help them determine the best facility for her.

Terrie asked the medics, "How is she?" They gave her the answer no one wants to hear. "You need to come to the hospital right away."

Terrie raced to the initial emergency room where they first took her mom. She coordinated with the EMTs and consoled her mother. The medical staff there explained that they'd be transferring her to another hospital with better facilities for traumatic brain injuries (TBI).

In our thirty-three years of marriage, this was, unfortunately, not the first time we'd had to respond to a family emergency. But Terrie was running out of family members. There was me, our son, and her mother. Terrie is the anchor of strength and peace, but I could tell it was different this time.

My wife is the kind of person that people are drawn to just because of the spirit and positive energy she exudes. I was going to be there for her, no matter what, just like it has always been and will always be.

TERRIE

Evening was falling. The hospital where they transported Mom is near the heart of downtown, about 20 miles from our home in the outer reaches of the big city. The March rain was cold and the emergency room was buzzing with doctors and nurses doing what they do best, while assorted families were sitting close together in the waiting room, deeply focused on hope and faith. We met with Mom in one of the emergency exam rooms.

She was sitting on the bed with her coat draped across her shoulders, dried blood on her clothes and face. Parts of her hair had been shaved away, exposing two very deep cuts, and one eye was already turning a deep shade of blue. One of the wounds was on her upper left forehead right at the hairline. The other was near the back left of her head. Both wounds looked horrible. She was obviously shaken, and the activity in the room and hallway seemed to frighten her. She said she was fine, but that her head sure hurt.

She had no recollection of what had happened and was wondering why everyone was fussing with her. I explained, again, that she had been in a car wreck and that she had bumped her head very badly.

We waited for hours for the neurosurgeon to bring us up to speed on the medical side of her injuries. As for any mental complications, we would just have to wait for the professionals to assess that for us. The surgeon expressed a lot of concern about head injuries. The images they took showed that her brain had contracted, leaving a space between the brain and her cranium.

Mom went into surgery so they could take a closer look and sew up her wounds, and we immediately called her boyfriend Billy to tell him what had happened. He was several hundred miles away in Ashland, Oregon serving as the bus driver for a high school field trip and said he would not be back for a few days. I was focused only on Mom's survival, but Jon's radar went into full alert. It just seemed odd that this man Mom loved didn't seem too concerned about the accident or her well-being. He made no attempt whatsoever to try and find assistance that would allow him to come and be with the woman he supposedly loved . . . my mother.

Billy made it clear that he was not going to make any attempt to get back to Portland sooner than he had planned, even though he knew that my mom was critically injured.

A nurse told us that she had been examined by Dr. Nguyen. She explained that he was one of the best neurosurgeons in town. He had cleaned her wounds up and ran a magnetic resonance imaging (MRI) scan on her so he could see the extent of her injury on the inside. The nurse introduced us to a new term, traumatic brain injury. Little did we know how much that term would mean to us in the future. She said Dr. Nguyen would return in the morning, so we just sat with Mom until late in the evening. When the sleep medicine had finally kicked in, we left for home, focused on hope and faith.

We went back to the hospital early the next day to find out the results of the MRI and have a chance to talk with the doctor. Mom was awake when we arrived.

The doctor had been in to see her and she had eaten some breakfast too, which seemed like a good sign! The doctor was a young man with dark hair, even shorter in stature than us, and a quick wit. He hurried in and sat down to give us the report.

He said that the MRI from last night showed some bleeding on the brain. He explained that with a TBI, the first twenty-four hours were critical. He said that they would be watching her closely for any signs in her mannerisms that things were worsening. He told us that with a TBI, the brain tightens up like a flinch when you bang your elbow.

Mom was seventy-five. The doctor explained that with the elderly, the brain may not return to normal as fast, which creates a space between the inside of the skull and the brain itself. The danger in having the space there is that it allows room for blood and other fluids to build up, causing pressure.

We talked with the nursing staff about TBI and tried to learn everything we could. It seemed that it was different for everybody. Some people returned to normal in weeks, some in months, some never.

They did say that the first year was usually when most of the healing came back, with steeply diminishing improvements after that. It really just depended on where the blunt force had struck the person and what, if anything, it had done to the brain. It was deeply concerning to us since there had been two separate points of impact.

The doctor had given us the police report, so we called the state patrol officer who was at the scene of the accident. Why? Because when something tragic happens to your loved one, you just want to know every detail and every piece of information in order to gain more control of at least knowing what you are dealing with. Control is an illusion, of course, because the event has already occurred. But sitting in the hospital room waiting on news of recovery, and what might come next, is a feeling of helplessness. So the natural reaction for us was to investigate, ask questions, and seek to understand.

The officer explained that mom had been traveling northbound on the interstate and was struck by another vehicle from the rear. He said that it appeared the other vehicle was traveling at a much higher rate of speed when he struck her, so the initial impact had caused her to hit her head the first time on the window post between the front and rear seat. Her vehicle then veered off of the freeway, where she struck a concrete barrier and hit her forehead on the wheel or dash.

Apparently, the airbag deployed on the first impact, so it was not as inflated by the time she hit the barrier. He said that she was unconscious when he arrived and was still unconscious when they took her in the ambulance. The officer sent me the full police report and the contact information for where they had towed her vehicle. The other driver had been taken to the emergency room and released later that day. We found out he was some sort of doctor associated with the first hospital, and we assumed that this was probably another reason why they had moved her to a different hospital.

Two days later, Mom still had no idea what had happened and was angry that she was being held in the hospital.

The more I tried to calm her, the more she became upset and confused. Mom kept asking where Billy was. She was testy all day. She did not want to be in the hospital and kept asking the same questions throughout the day. I bought her some easy crossword puzzles, because she always loved to do those. But now, she could not get the answers. She did not seem frustrated and simply put whatever word or portion of word that came to mind into the boxes. The nurses said it would take a few days to know what damage had been caused by the shock of the trauma and what her real mental status was.

I told Mom that Billy was out of town and would be back in a few days.

On the fourth day that Mom was in the hospital, we started seeing that her cognitive functions were severely hampered. She couldn't remember what had been said to her minutes earlier. Basic testing from the hospital staff showed that she wasn't able to perform simple tasks such as looking at a clock and telling the time. In fact, she couldn't even tell what number each hand was pointing at.

I knew then that she would never be the same.

CHAPTER 2

Jon

We spent many hours at the hospital for the next few days. Jean, Terrie's Mom, became more frustrated as the days went by. She still did not remember the wreck or why she was there. The hospital social workers started doing some simple cognitive testing each day to determine what functions had been affected and to note any improvements in those areas. Jean couldn't perform the tests very well, which frustrated her even more.

The testing consisted of having Jean remember recent and long-ago events. Her long-term memory seemed pretty good except for approximate years of when things happened. Her short-term cognitive functions were very poor. She kept saying that this all seemed like a dream that she could not wake up from.

Terrie tried her best to comfort her, but Jean was so resistant to her efforts. Jean did not want to be waited on or consoled. She wanted to do everything herself, but at the same time did not have the mental faculties to actually perform the tasks. Jean asked for something to read, so Terrie bought her some magazines. It appeared that Jean could not read very well right now, and could not tell us anything about what she had just read.

After five days in the hospital, continued MRIs showed that her head trauma was not getting worse, but not getting better either. The doctor said that she could check out, but that she needed twenty-four-hour care. She was not to do anything physically demanding and she was not to bend over.

The doctor was quite concerned about Jean hitting her head in any way. We talked with the hospital social workers about caring for someone in her condition. They were not as helpful as we would have liked. With a TBI being different for everybody, they could not tell us what to expect, but also did not explain to us how impaired her cognitive function was, as explained earlier. We asked about in-home care services and they handed us a sheet of paper that had the names of some people who performed in-home care.

The names were just written out with phone numbers, instead of something you would expect to have been professionally produced, given that there are so many people with head injuries. They said there were franchised in-home care companies as well, but they were extremely expensive. Terrie and I discussed our very limited options and decided that we would have Jean stay in our home for the time being.

This way, we could closely monitor her and make sure she had what she needed, like a good diet, a clean environment, and her family close by to comfort her. We also decided that for us to be able to be caretakers and continue to work, we needed to divide tasks. Terrie would be in charge of taking care of Jean's needs, as Terrie could work her business from home. I would be in charge of setting up insurances, finding an accident attorney, taking care of the wrecked car, and any other tasks regarding professional services.

I started doing as much Internet research about TBIs as I could. It seemed there was hardly any long-term testing of this injury. Studies showed there was a lot of conflicting data because brain studies, while much improved, were still in the frontier stages. There were recent studies being conducted around professional football players, and they were finding that retired players were experiencing severe mental deficiencies and early death. In fact, there is currently a lawsuit against the National Football League claiming damages for concussions which were apparently not taken as seriously as the team doctors should taken them. You know: "You're fine, get out there and play!" We are seeing much more testing these days with the advanced equipment used in sports, but the long-term testing will take many years.

Symptoms would appear to doctors as various types of dementia such as Alzheimer's, leading doctors in that field of study not to connect it to head injuries, thus leading to the tug-of-war for doctors to make new discoveries. It was evident in reviewing medical reports from professionals working with dementia patients that we were dealing with something much more difficult, although communicating with dementia patients seemed close to what we were experiencing with Jean, with the patient not being able to remember much of anything happening in the here and now.

I was able to locate an accident attorney with a sterling record of success. His services were extremely steep from a cost perspective, but still consistent with how others were charging for their services. He and I had several lengthy conversations so he could get all of the information he needed. He sent his people to examine Jean's car and retrieve personal items left there. When we saw the pictures they had taken, the severity of the collision became much more clear to us. The car was a total loss.

I want to make a clear distinction in vocabulary regarding car wrecks. They are commonly referred to as "accidents," but that is only due to the marketing and wordsmith professionals in the insurance industry, who seek to make wrecks seem not as bad, in their advertising, as they often really are. This type of redirect marketing is also carried on by the car manufacturers as they create commercials showing how fast their car can go and how quickly their car gets to a certain speed.

They depict cars flying, jumping onto trains, how quiet their cars are, how many technical distractions they can build into their cars. Then there are the cute things like mascots, or animals talking about a certain car. "Oh how cute, I want that car!" Very seldom do you hear of car safety ratings, except for those manufacturers who build with safety in mind. In fact, General Motors recently made the largest recall in automotive history. Most of those vehicles recalled were for faulty ignition switches, a problem which was known about for a decade, but apparently covered up by company officials.

Make no mistake they are wrecks, not accidents. They are tragic, ugly, and bring such debilitating grief to families every hour of every day. While I wrote this paragraph, at least one family somewhere was just finding out that a loved one had been killed or seriously injured in a car wreck. Their lives will be negatively impacted forever.

When it comes to car wrecks, the truth is that someone made a poor choice or was not paying attention, which in itself is a poor choice. There is nearly always fault found in at least one of the drivers; this is not by accident. This is negligence. Just as with GM, someone made a poor choice.

Terrie lost her only brother in a car wreck when we were thirty years old. It was not an accident, because a lady in a van made a poor choice and turned in front of him and his car was stuffed under the van, killing him instantly. Terrie's brother was an incredibly talented person, too. He was the state snare drum champion all four years of high school and had every potential to do so much with his music for the world to see—until that lady turned her van into a weapon.

BACK HOME

We eventually had Jean comfortably situated in our home. The day-to-day care was difficult but manageable. Terrie would include Jean in as many daily tasks as possible. For instance, she would have Jean help with dinner preparation and cleanup. But these tasks were so very difficult and frustrating for Jean. She could not do a place setting properly, could not load the dishwasher, could not understand a recipe, or figure out which measuring cup was the right one. Many times, Jean would start crying and go to her room. There was no consoling her at these times.

Terrie regularly took Jean to the occupational therapist. The therapist would do more of the cognitive testing. Jean would be completely stressed out prior to any appointment because she wanted to get better and showing she could do the tests would prove that. Unfortunately, she would do very poorly. The therapist was very encouraging to Jean and would praise her for trying as hard as she did. Jean would take some comfort when we all praised her, but at times she would take that to mean she was getting better, and that was not the case in the slightest. Terrie would also take Jean to her own house to do some cleaning and to allow Terrie to organize Jean's office.

One day she heard Jean say, "Oh, I think I made a mistake." When Terrie went to her she found that Jean had removed one of her shoestrings and was wearing it like a necklace. When Terrie returned home, she was visibly shaking. She told me what had happened and started to cry. I held her close and reassured her she was doing the best she could. Terrie is not one to expose emotions like that, and I knew the situation was starting to get to her.

We arranged for friends of Jean's to come and stay with her at her house from time to time so that we could catch up on our work and go have dinner somewhere, just the two of us. This arrangement worked well except that even the friends would have a difficult time communicating with her, and Jean would be very dramatic about her anguish in wanting to be well again.

Terrie took Jean to the doctor for a regular appointment. She gave him the documentation the doctor had asked her to keep and also a sheet of concerns that she noted occurred with Jean after the accident. He told Jean that the brain would take some time to recover and that she shouldn't worry too much about the forgetfulness or absentmindedness. He said that it could take upwards of six weeks to get back to normal and possibly longer in older people.

He showed them the CT scans and where they had first seen blood on the brain. He also showed them an area of concern around the outer edge of the brain. He said that fluid could develop in that area and, if so, it might require an operation to drain the fluid. He said that Jean could get a CT scan now just to see if there was any difference, and then most likely get another one in May. He referenced President Reagan and his fall from his horse as an example. He said that Jean still needed to be with us for at least another month because he wanted her with someone.

The doctor said that she could spend time by herself, could spend time with her boyfriend, and that she could travel as long as she had someone with her. He also told her no bending, heavy lifting, or hard exercise yet. Going home in the car, Jean said that she was glad the doctor had told her about the forgetfulness and absentmindedness. She said, "Now I can forgive myself more." She also said she wasn't ready to do too much yet because it all got overwhelming when she tried to think things through.

We contacted an attorney who specializes in elder law. His name was Todd, a middle-aged man running his own practice after years in larger firms. Todd was a very soft-spoken man who worked in an office that was spotlessly organized, complete with pictures of his family and pets.

We wanted to find out if there was anything we might be overlooking and generally wanted to find out what our future options might be if Jean did not improve. Todd was very thorough in explaining how conservatorship and guardianship worked. Neither one seemed to come into play, but we wanted to be sure we were doing things the right way. We mentioned our concerns regarding Billy, but Todd felt we just needed to focus on Jean, and that he was pretty sure Billy would not be around much longer once he saw that Jean was not going to be her usual self any more. Todd also said that if Billy hadn't done anything illegal, there wasn't really anything we could do anyway. It was a relief to hear from a professional that he thought we were doing such a great job under the extreme circumstances.

Three weeks after leaving the hospital to come live with us to recover, Jean came out of her room one day and asked, "Do you think I'm walking funny?"

We both watched her walk back and forth through the living room in a very unsteady way. Terrie noted that she was walking strangely, and I asked Jean if she was dizzy. She said, "Not really, just kind of foggy." We had her sit down and Terrie called the doctor immediately.

The doctor said to bring her in right away for another MRI, so Terrie drove her to the hospital for that test. The doctor reviewed the MRI results and said there was additional fluid building up in the space around her brain. He wanted Terrie to bring her mom back in a few days to have another MRI performed.

The doctor also told Terrie to have a bag packed for Jean

because, if the test showed another increase of fluid, he would want to admit her to the hospital and perform surgery right away.

CHAPTER 3

Terrie

After the accident my mother was extremely forgetful. She had difficulty with simple things, like following directions on a cake mix or putting things together in the right order. She couldn't figure out what day it was, even as she looked at a calendar and obsessed over it for long periods of time.

Her real obsessive focus centered on her boyfriend, Billy.

She wasn't the happy, bubbly person she used to be and she knew it. She'd often say to me, "I just don't feel like myself anymore." Mom became easily agitated and frustrated. She wanted to be able to think, remember, and do like she'd done before the accident, but she couldn't. It frustrated her to no end because before the accident she had always been such a perfectionist.

After the accident, she couldn't do things in the same way as she used to, no matter how hard she tried.

JON

I found myself looking back, before the accident, recalling conversations and actions in an effort to connect all the dots. Years after Terrie's father died, her mother started dating Billy, and when we had asked about him she always talked fondly of him. Before the accident, Jean would come over every week for dinner on Sundays, and as time passed the relationship seemed to grow stronger to the point where Jean would sometimes skip Sunday dinner to be with him. After a couple of years of this relationship, we started to ask when we were going to meet Billy.

For some reason, Jean was always a bit non-committal about making a plan for us to meet him. She said that Billy was a very "private" person. I started to feel suspicious of this man, as though he had something to hide rather than just being a private person. After another year passed, we were concerned that we hadn't been introduced to him, and Terrie pressed Jean to set a meeting.

Personally, I had my suspicions about a man who wouldn't honor a request to meet with the children of the woman he was dating for a long period of time. We had a background check performed on him, which turned up very little except that he had no money, was divorced twice, worked as a school bus driver, and lived in a pole barn with a living area built into it. My suspicions grew.

Finally, one day, Jean and Billy came to our home. Billy was very quiet. I looked him in the eyes and asked him, "So, I'm wondering why it has taken you so long to meet with us?" He looked down at his feet and said, "I don't need another family, I have a family of my own."

This was my first real 'aha' moment that boiled up through my gut, screaming that something was very wrong with this man and his intentions regarding Jean. I said nothing and continued to look at him while he stared at his feet. He finally looked at me for a second and quickly turned his gaze toward his feet again. I knew then that I was not looking at a man with honor. He was more like a dog that comes sniffing around the back door at night.

He was a lonely, self-absorbed man with nothing to show for his life. One who visited senior social circles, hunting for a wealthy trophy wife who would fall for his smooth talk and pay for anything his heart desired. My suspicions confirmed, I considered what this might mean for Jean and us as time moved forward.

I discussed my feelings with Terrie, but she didn't see it that way. She was a loving daughter and wanted to see her mom happy. I also wanted Jean to be happy, but the way she was fawning over this guy like a little girl made my danger radar go to full alert. Terrie and I discussed this several more times. In the end, I told her that I knew something was wrong, but respected her wishes and wouldn't press the issue any further. However, I did tell Terrie that I felt this was going to turn into something bad one day and that we wouldn't be happy about it. You know how you just have a gut feeling about someone?

That was my initial instinct early on. Things didn't seem right.

TERRIE'S VIEW

After the accident, Mom needed therapy. When I walked in one day, eager to be supportive, I suddenly got a very clear impression that my mom didn't want me there and I knew something was really wrong. As the weeks went on I had been sensing that she seemed to be more and more distrusting of me, but I couldn't understand why. I was her daughter, and I'd been there for her all along.

I went so far as to call Billy because my mother and I had always had a trusting relationship and now it seemed so different.

I called and asked him why she seemed so angry and distrusting of me. Billy told me that it was because Jon and I were the first ones to see her after the surgery, when she was hurting and angry. He said that she blamed us. It was confusing, and it didn't make any sense at all.

What the doctor was seeing in the latest MRI from Mom was that there was no brain expansion yet and that there was a buildup of blood and fluids in that space between her brain and her skull. This is referred to as a subdural hematoma. The blood and fluids are just the body's way of reacting to the injury, but if the buildup becomes too much, the patient can die. If the blood starts to coagulate around the brain, it can form a web-type structure that does not allow the brain to bounce back to fill the space and can cause so much pressure that the brain reacts by shutting down.

The doctor said he was going to perform a Burr Hole Trephination first, but if that did not look like it was functioning properly he would have to do the Craniotomy in order to see what was happening. Instead of waiting until the next day to do the surgery, Mom was admitted immediately to the hospital and the surgery was performed that evening. We waited until late into the night so we could be there when the surgery was complete and we could get a report from the doctor.

Hospital workers must see people like us pass through their professional lives all of the time. Family members wandering the halls, talking with staff, keeping children busy, holding each other in silence, buying food in the cafeteria, stirring cold food and not finishing their dinner . . . again. Then they are gone and other families fill the void. It is never ending for them, but they are so polite, respectful, and compassionate toward our plight.

The doctor came out and told us the surgery went very well and the Trephination surgery looked like it was working. Mom would be in the intensive care unit so she could be monitored closely, and another MRI would be performed the following day. We returned home early in the morning knowing we both had our jobs to attend to at first light and then back to the hospital once we had finished urgent work and pushed back items that could wait until another time. It was an emotional night. Jon and I lay in bed and just held each other until sleep relieved us from the torment of our thoughts.

When we first saw Mom the next day, the sight was quite horrific. She was sitting up in her intensive care unit bed and was awake. She had four tubes extending out of the top of her head and a huge dressing surrounding the tubes resembling a turban. Because she had struck both the front and back of her head, the doctor had to drill extra holes so that they could flush the entire surface of her brain. They pumped in the solution through two of the holes; it swirled around and then exited the other two tubes, emptying into containers under her bed. She was not happy at all to be there. She seemed more alert than she had been and knew she had been in a car wreck. She was so very worried about her condition and having to be in the hospital. She cried softly and I tried to console her, but she was also mad! Mad at the situation, mad at the guy who had run into her, even mad at me for some reason. She was very snippy when I tried to make her more comfortable, or asked her if she needed water or anything. You couldn't read anything into her behavior because she was damaged so badly. She was a shell of her former self, and she knew it.

JON'S VIEW

My relationship with Jean started when Terrie and I met and started dating. We were sophomores in high school at the time, just sixteen years old. Terrie's family was a typical suburban family, I suppose. Her dad was a career high school music teacher, and her mother was a career elementary school music teacher. Terrie's only sibling was her younger brother Gregg, who was an aspiring drummer just entering high school. At that time, I was doing just fine with grades and had many extracurricular activities. It was the early 1970s, and even with my long hair of the times I was on the high school cross country and wrestling teams, and was also racing outdoor motocross every weekend. I was very energetic!

I was very respectful to Terrie's parents and did everything I could to stay in their good graces. Terrie was never home late from a date and that was a very good thing in her dad's eyes. I became a part of the family, so to speak, as Terrie and I were inseparable. I went with them to family outings and even on some of their vacations. Gregg and I hit it off well; he liked motorcycles too, so he would come to races and later he would get a motorcycle and we would ride together at the family's vacation property on the high desert of central Oregon.

Terrie and I married five years later, when we were each twenty-one, and had our son about a year and a half later. We would go to Sunday dinner at her parents' house every week. Jean was a stickler about those dinners; it was family time and the only times we did not go was for a preplanned event of some type. We celebrated every birthday and every holiday together. Christmas was a three-day event of food and gifts, more gifts and more food. Even my parents were a part of this family time. My two sisters lived out of state, so my parents would celebrate with us and Terrie's parents.

I admired Jean in so many ways. She was a working professional and homemaker. She was a very Christian woman who was devout to her church and religion. She volunteered for the teachers' association and the church. We never had cross words with each other, and she is one who would not hold back if she had something to say!

Terrie's only brother was killed in a car wreck when we were about thirty. Her mom and dad took it very hard, as one might imagine, and I was asked by her parents to be a pallbearer at the funeral. They never pressed charges or filed a lawsuit against the lady who killed him, which I thought was odd. I believe that people need to hold accountable those who perpetrate crimes against us, even unintentionally, and this was manslaughter at the very least. Terrie and I still visit his grave at Christmas and on his birthday every year.

As I moved into corporate leadership roles for work, none of our traditions changed; we were a tight family. Then Terrie's dad died of heart failure. We were at our coastal vacation home about 100 miles away, and drove quickly in the middle of the night to be there for Jean. When we arrived at the hospital, Terrie's dad was just barely holding on, and we had just a short time to talk to him before his body started shutting down. Jean was a mess of conflicted feelings and really could not think straight. They did not have an advanced medical directive, and once his body had shut down, Jean had to decide when it was time to "pull the plug," so to speak. As for most anyone, this is a situation you do not want to be in. After the doctors had explained that he was purely on life support with no hope of regaining consciousness, Jean made the decision to move forward. The hospital moved him to a private room and Terrie, her mom, and I joined him there and waited. After a couple of hours, he breathed his last breath. I remember Jean crying uncontrollably next to the bed, with Terrie hugging her, and me holding Terrie's hand. I was so thankful we could be there for him and for each other.

TERRIE

After we had moved Mom back into her home, things only got worse. Whenever I would call her, she had nothing to say. I would ask her questions about what she'd been doing and she'd ask why I was asking. I'd tell her that I was only trying to make conversation. I was only concerned for her well-being and happiness.

In mid-May, we were scheduled to have an appointment with Mom and her financial advisor, Sherrie. We had met with her several times since the accident. When I got there, I could see that Mom had been to the bank, most likely with one of the caregivers.

There were bank statements on the table and I could see that she had been writing all over them. There was one check that I'd written for her to the IRS in the amount of twelve thousand dollars, and she wanted to know what that was for. I tried to explain it several different ways, and Sherrie tried to explain that it was money she owed the IRS, but she didn't understand. Mom thought that check shouldn't have been written, and argued with us.

To say the least, it wasn't a good meeting. In the end, Sherrie said that she would come by every week if Mom wanted help understanding her finances. She also told Jean that she thought I should be put on her accounts for the time being, but Mom wouldn't allow that.

She said that she'd had so much taken away from her since the accident that she was going to keep control of her finances. Sherrie told her that until she got better, that was the last thing she should keep control of. Mom wouldn't budge. We left Mom's house, and before I could pull out of the driveway Sherrie called and said that she felt I should start the conservatorship process right away.

Sherrie saw some serious red flags . . .

CHAPTER 4

Jon

Wolves are natural predators, and often isolate their prey.

It's a smart hunting strategy, because they can then focus on the easiest kill. Ranchers often use donkeys, or livestock guard dogs, to help alert the humans and protect their pasture animals from the wolf.

After Billy had been at our house the first time, we began to observe how he was isolating Terrie's mom, and neither one had any interest in spending time with her family or communicating with us whatsoever.

In fact, none of Jean's closest friends, church parishioners, professional team members, or other family members had ever met Billy until after the accident. We would come to learn that isolation is the best way to unduly influence the vulnerable and control outside interactions.

I was the one who looked into Billy's background even

though my wife never would have thought of doing such a thing. All I could learn about him was that he had a minor warrant in another county for an unpaid traffic violation. He had lived in Alaska for several years and had been divorced twice. His home was a pole barn with an apartment-type living space inside that was registered in his sister's name. I continued to search, the way any protector would. If it were a daughter, or a friend, and you felt like you were losing them, you'd want to reach out, discover what you could about the predator's background, and help rescue your loved one.

I felt like Billy was a predator. He used a post office box and his property sat back off of the road unseen, although Google Earth allows one to see quite a bit. I looked for his house and saw a small pole barn, isolated back off the road. Terrie just wanted a relationship back. We could see things sliding. I wanted to know why. I wanted to know what Billy was up to. I had sensed something bad from the start.

True, this was Terrie's mother being victimized, but after thirty-one years of marriage and thirty-six years of knowing Jean from the age of 16, this was happening to both of us. She was my family, too.

After Terrie's father passed, Jean continued to volunteer for the teachers' association when she retired, and became even more involved with helping the church out as much as possible. We introduced the Elder Hostel organization to Jean, and she went on several of their organized group trips around the country. These trips really helped her break out into her own again. I would help Jean around the house when she needed and talked to contractors when there were more major repairs required. The three of us would go get Christmas trees together every year, and I would help her get it set up and put up all of the outdoor Christmas lights for her. I enjoyed helping her out and never felt these were chores, just something that family did.

CHAPTER 5

Jon

Psychopaths often isolate and brainwash their victims, and it can happen in an instant . . . to you, to me, to anyone we love.

How Billy culled her out is beyond us. Was she an easy target? Did he see her as a frail woman, and target her for her companionship, or money? Her day-to-day life was something we now realize we had no knowledge of. As a son-in-law who loved and supported his mother-in-law, it was hard for me to accept, but of course it was much harder for my wife.

Jean used to remind me of the actress Betty White. She was vibrant and full life, yet after the accident, and a brain injury, it was the perfect storm for Billy to move in and take over even more.

TERRIE

In the years prior to Mom's accident, I had only met Billy

three times. Once when he came to our house, and then two other times when I knew he was at Mom's house and I made an excuse to have to stop by, but each of those times was just for a few minutes, so I really couldn't get any sense of him, other than he seemed nice enough. I thought it was really weird that he didn't join us at least for holidays; it so went against the grain of our family history. I was hurt by that. None of Mom's professional people ever met Billy. Before the accident few, if any, of Mom's friends had met Billy.

In fact, one of her friends whom she'd known for more than 30 years said to me that she used to think Mom was just making Billy up because she never brought him to meet her circle of friends. After the wreck I saw him briefly a few times in the hospital. I asked him several times to please call me if he had any questions or concerns relating to Mom, but he never did. By the time I saw his true colors it was too late; our lives were in a tailspin.

A CONVINCING PREDATOR

The gravity of Billy's influence, not only on my Mother, but on law enforcement and legal professionals, was mind-blowing. My first realization of this came when I called my Mom's cell phone because I needed to have her sign some papers for the long-term care insurance company. A police officer answered her phone.

She identified herself as Officer Powers. She said that there was a situation at Mom's house and that Mom was accusing me of stealing large amounts of money from her. I was horrified, and terrified! She said Mom didn't want to talk to me and that Billy was there taking care of her. The officer said that if I'd been doing my responsibility while I was taking care of my mother's finances, I'd have an accounting of all of the monies. She wanted the ledger I'd been keeping. She told me I wouldn't have to worry about anything if I gave it to her, that it would prove my innocence. We made arrangements that I would give it to her the next week. I hung up in disbelief; I couldn't believe what I'd just heard. My own Mother was accusing me of stealing from her!

I talked to the officer again one more time before hiring an attorney. I explained to her that I was worried about Billy's influence over my mother. I thought that he was involved in this somehow. But the officer said that she thought that they were a cute, doting couple and very sweet. She said that this was just like one of her nephews who was taking money from some relative and the other family members didn't like it, but there was nothing they could do. I told her it was nothing like that at all.

No matter what I said, Officer Powers' mind was made up. In fact, during a future conversation with my attorney, she told him that she believed that I had stolen the money from my mother.

DESCENT INTO ISOLATION

Then Mom's financial advisor Sherrie called. She asked what was going on, and I said I didn't know because the police officer told me not to call over there, and I hadn't. Sherrie said that Mom had called and told her that she was changing financial advisors. She said that Mom was very short with her, and hung up on her. She said that she would try to slow the process down, but that Mom could technically do whatever she wanted.

We called Mom's estate attorney, Bill Best, and told him about what Sherrie had relayed to us. We told him that we felt that Billy was strategically, systematically turning her against everyone. First it was Jon, then me, then Sherrie. He said that was too bad because Sherrie was the one element that we really needed. He said that he'd talked with Jack Grimes, the accident attorney, and when Jack had called Mom there was a female who was telling her what to say. We told him that was the caregiver, Marge, most likely.

Marge called and said the police officer had said that she could no longer talk to me. She said that Billy was now power of attorney and that they'd faxed those papers to the doctors that day. She explained that Billy was instructing the senior care company now, and she said that she told him she couldn't do anything unless she saw a revised power of attorney (POA) document. Marge said that he was spending the nights with her, and he wanted a caregiver there in the event he didn't stay. She said that Mom's anxiety was very high even though she was taking her meds.

We called Todd, the elder law attorney we had met with shortly after the accident, to get some answers and see what our options were. He said that the guardianship/conservatorship process could be put on the fast track, but if she were to fight it, it could take up to four months. Due to the complexity of the case, he referred us to a man named Matt Downs, and he suggested we contact the county Elder Protection Division, which we did. The wheels were now in motion.

We spoke with a gentleman named Ron at Elder Protection and told him the story. Listening to our version of the story, he concluded the situation was a mess and that he didn't think that someone could be allowed to take over POA if the person wasn't fully competent.

The trouble was Billy had managed to convince the right people that she was fully competent. We knew better. So we now knew what we needed to prove, that she was not fully aware, or in control of the situation.

We told Ron that we couldn't get a letter from the doctor because they told him not to talk to me. He said that we definitely had a case; he just wasn't sure whether it would be on the financial side or the custodial side. It felt so jarring talking about my mother in this way. It was so messed up. He concluded that we needed to get an attorney. It certainly looked like criminal mischief to him.

I called my uncle and aunt to bring them up to speed on the situation, and they said that Billy had called them the past Sunday for the first time ever. Billy told him that I was trying to move my mother into assisted living and take all of her money. Luckily, my uncle had the good sense to tell him that I would never do such a thing. He then told Billy he thought he was trying to take all of Mom's money. Mom had shared with my uncle that she'd paid for their trip to Alaska and that she'd given Billy money at other times too. My uncle told Billy to never call there again and hung up.

JOINED IN MATRIMONY

It was about 2:30 in the afternoon of July 8th, less than a week since the police involvement, when I heard the phone ring. I went to it and could see on the caller ID that it was Mom, so I answered.

She said, "Hi Terrie, this is Mom. I just wanted to let you know that I have some great news. Billy and I just got married; congratulations are in order. I'll talk to you about it later." She then hung up.

It was as if she didn't realize that I had even answered the phone, like she was just leaving a message. I was devastated and in shock.

I called Jon for consolation. I called my uncle and aunt, who were appalled. I texted Sherrie, who was on vacation, and I called my son, who said, "I knew something like this would happen." I called and left a message with the Elder Protection investigator and Matt, the new attorney.

We would later learn that Billy had flown my mother, and her caregiver to Las Vegas, married her, and flew back the next day. I felt disgusted and somehow violated.

I called Matt and told him the whole story. I was scared, really scared. At the end of that phone call he agreed to represent me. I met with him several days later, and he warned me that I was going to be receiving restraining orders soon, coming from my mother and Billy.

In other conversations with Matt, he told me that Elder Protective Services were actually investigating me! He wasn't too happy with them as he didn't feel that I should be the focus of a witch hunt when I hadn't done anything wrong. He said Billy should have never been able to get a restraining order based only on allegations, but Billy's powers of persuasion were proving successful, and when Matt talked to the police officer, she admitted that she did believe that I was stealing money.

OUT OF MY HANDS

The whole experience with my mother was worse than experiencing a death in the family. With deaths one feels great pain and sadness, that a family member is missed so much, but over time, that fades to more manageable emotions. This experience was a whole new level of daily hell. Fear characterized each day —over and over and over again.

Jon was so supportive, I know he was terribly afraid too. We didn't know what was going to happen next. The only thing we could count on to get through this was each other. Our son, and my aunt and uncle, were supportive too, but they didn't have to go through the minute-to-minute things we were dealing with and feeling. I can remember sitting on the back porch just being there together with Jon trying to make sense of what was happening to us. I couldn't have made it through that ordeal without him. He was my rock, even though he was just as scared as I was. He loved my mother. I think we both withdrew from the regular world, which didn't seem regular at all anymore. I was withdrawn at work, didn't talk much to anyone. I cried a lot. I couldn't believe what was happening and I couldn't talk to my mother. We couldn't sleep, couldn't eat; I was paralyzed in emotional pain. Living through the whole ordeal was the worst part of my life.

CHAPTER 6

Terrie

Throughout the aftermath of learning that my mother had a boyfriend who had taken over her life, the few people who knew the story asked me how I was handling it. It's not really something you "handle." You just get through and try to find answers.

JON

This entire process was frustrating because we had absolutely no control. The justice system has its rules and the process moves at a slow, lumbering pace, with the lawyers dancing the dance of courtroom policy and politics.

We have learned that anybody can take anyone to court for anything. If there hadn't been a Trust in our family, we would not have had the legal right to do anything. We only have limited answers on how Billy was able to take over Jean's life. It was done with shocking speed. It happened all in one week.

In a nutshell, Billy did what all predators do and painted a really good picture. The police officer, who bought Billy's story without proof, apparently guided them through the process of filing a restraining order and going to protective services. The next week, Billy hired a caretaker and flew Jean to Vegas, married her, and flew back the next day. They then applied for restraining orders against us. Billy hit the jackpot. Jean had a tidy nest egg of money. Teachers generally don't make large sums of money . . . but as a retired teacher her PERS benefits and Social Security benefits made for a comfortable monthly wage. In addition, Jean's father had bought land and mineral rights in the Midwest that had been passed on to family. The oil drilling had begun several years ago and was now paying off in the thousands each month.

Our new elder law attorney, Matt, was a godsend. After being bounced from one referral to the next because of scheduling conflicts, Matt came into our lives. He practices elder law, but most always represents the elderly party in his cases. He took our case because he was aware of some of the gray areas in elder law and how these had all come into play with us.

Matt is a middle-aged man with a stocky build. A suit-and-tie professional working in a large firm, with his own caseload, as well as litigating cases for others in the firm. He is one who honestly cares about what he does and takes extra care to explain how the laws apply and that what one may think should happen does not always apply. Throughout our ordeal I had pushed Matt pretty hard at times through my own frustration with the situation. Matt never discounted any items I had presented to him, but rather talked me off of the proverbial ledge and gave me consolation through understanding my point of view. I have the greatest respect for Matt, but I am certainly a person who wants to make sure the course of action is the very best one. With so many professionals failing in their duties to this point, I just wanted to make extra sure.

TERRIE

Matt was so upset at what had transpired thus far. He was very familiar with Officer Powers, and also knew the judge who granted the restraining orders. He was dumbfounded that the judge had issued that orders without proof, and said that she was a well-respected and usually very thorough judge. As Matt lined out the process we would have to follow, he explained that the first order of business was to get the restraining orders rescinded, and then we could pursue a hearing to have a court-appointed conservator put in place to handle Mom's financial affairs.

When we went to the first hearing it was the first time we'd seen Mom in over eight months. It was kind of surreal being in that type of environment, seeing her and not being able to talk with her.

Seven months earlier, Mom's new attorney, Mr. Cook, told Matt that if I didn't try to call her they'd drop the restraining orders, which they did. He also liked to threaten that they wouldn't change the Trust if I would comply. I never could understand what right Mr. Cook thought he had to come into our lives and try to change what my mother and father had put together for our future. He never even knew my mother before the accident, so he didn't know what her wishes were. I can only believe that his motives were for his own financial gain. I've always wanted to ask him that; I want to know why he worked so hard to destroy my relationship with my mother. Who put him in charge of our family matters? Well, now I know the answer to that: Billy put him in charge. You see, Mr. Cook had represented Billy in other legal matters prior to Billy meeting my mother. Now, Mr. Cook was representing my mother!

When we saw Mom at the hearing, she was heavier than when I'd last seen her. She was dressed casually, too casually for a court appearance. Mom always used to look so nice. She was particular about her clothes, and her outfits were always nicely put together with jackets and sweaters. Yet that day she was dressed in a button-down shirt and jeans. She was also using a cane, which I thought was very strange. My Mother, with the exception of arthritis in her hands, had always been physically fit. Before the accident she went to the gym three times a week. So why was she now using a cane? Or, was Mr. Cook making her out to look frail?

Billy and Mr. Cook had obviously told her not to look at me, or perhaps she didn't recognize me? Even when I was testifying on the stand she didn't look at me. We never made eye contact even though I was looking directly at her several times. Inside the courtroom Mr. Cook sat between us with my attorney Matt to my right. It was a surreal experience. I could never have imagined that I'd be sitting at a table in a courtroom with my Mother just a person away and attorneys arguing whether or not she was subject to undue financial influence and needed a conservator.

The court process is horrible, but in some ways I didn't mind going because I got to see a glimpse of my mother. Yet even in those glimpses, I realized it was a prison of sorts, as if you were a family member visiting an inmate, your loved one, who had been sentenced to life. It was a sudden realization that I would never have my mother again, even though she was alive. I would never hug her, or restore the relationship we'd had, because she was no longer there.

Mom had been brainwashed to believe that we were bad, unloving people. She wouldn't go see her other family, or even talk to her grandson. In fact, she had to ask Billy if she even had a grandson.

JON

When we went into the courtroom, it was obvious that Jean was not well.

She seemed very confused about what was going on or where to sit. She didn't even know anymore that she was to rise when the judge came in.

There were several other people there with her at the courthouse that day. We had no idea who they were, but obviously they were either friends or family of Billy. They were fawning around her and laughing. More vultures coming to pick the bones of the mentally disabled woman Billy had conquered.

Terrie and Jean had been extremely close, so of course it was all terribly difficult to watch unfold.

CHAPTER 7

Terrie

Prior to the wreck, I thought that I was the person closest to my mother, and that's how it was for the longest time. We were a close family. My parents were both music teachers, so we had the summers off. We did a lot of traveling, camping mostly, and would spend a couple weeks every summer at my grandparents' cabin on a lake in North Dakota. Sunday night was always family night. We had dinner together, played games, or watched a little TV. Sunday night family night lasted into my adult years and throughout my marriage with Jon. We had dinner together with my parents almost every Sunday until my dad's death in 2002.

After my brother's death we celebrated his birthday every year. It was a tribute to his memory . . . but that stopped with Mom's wreck. When my dad died, Mom and I became even closer. I'd talk to her almost every evening. She was really lonely. Jon and I took her places with us, and Sunday night family night was now at our home. She didn't like to stay in her house much as it was so big. It had four levels and way too much space for her, but she couldn't sell it either; too many memories were there. Mom loved her things, family furniture that had been passed down through the generations, and there was a lot of it which she would have to part with had she sold the house. So she never did.

Before Dad's death Christmas was always a cherished time. Mom and I made batches of Christmas cookies together for years, and we continued on with that tradition even after Dad passed, right up until the accident. Mom and I used to meet for coffee once a week, and there was nothing we kept from each other. I even helped her with some financial decisions as she grew older. These were all now distant memories of a woman I used to know.

Growing up, we were a close family. It wasn't quite like a Norman Rockwell painting, but we had two loving parents and grandparents. We weren't rich, teachers generally are not. But we did a lot, more than most as far as going on trips and seeing new sights. My parents really loved each other; sure, they'd argue now and then. I can remember clearly my dad saying, "Geez, Jean!"

My mom wasn't without her own set of issues, either. She was actually hospitalized when I was still in grade school for what I think was a nervous breakdown. She was gone for a month. We'd take her from the hospital on Sunday, go for a drive and then out to lunch, and then drive her back. I learned as an adult that she'd had numerous electroshock therapy sessions. It didn't seem to hinder her spirit though, as she was always a woman with a can-do attitude. Once she made up her mind, that was it. She sang a lot, as did her mother, and you could always tell she was happy if she was singing.

She didn't sing much after my dad died. And that's why I had been so open to a new man in her life. To anything, really, that would bring back her joy.

CHAPTER 8

Jon

Any tragedy or obstacle your spouse faces is yours, too.

Whether it's financial, family, or illness, many people start the blame game. Since each one of us responds to a problem differently, the responses tend to be varied, and can be divisive. We've seen many marriages shattered by illness, death, or financial strain. When we reached our worst breaking point, I responded to the stress by continuing to hold my love for Terrie in the highest regard, while we both tried with everything we could muster to maintain some semblance of sanity.

The cosmic injustice, my wife's grief, my grief, the immoral acts committed by Billy, the failure of public servants to do their job . . . I felt a part of me break. But I also knew I had to hold it together somehow for the long road ahead of us.

If you are married, you understand that if your spouse has

a financial crisis, a personal crisis, or a work crisis, it's yours too. Many marriages fall apart during these difficult trials. Ours didn't. I suppose some would consider this book a part of our legacy, although we really don't care about such things in the big picture of life. It is our hope that in some way our story will help others pull together and take the steps necessary to protect their own family.

As we began to see Terrie's mother just slipping farther and farther away, it was a helpless feeling. What would you do if someone you knew, and loved, had been brainwashed by another human to hate you? *Hate* is a strong word, but ultimately that's what it amounted to. We lost all contact with Jean.

Terrie and I melded into each other deeper than I think most couples can even imagine. We talked together, cried together, remained sleepless and not hungry together, and worked with our professional team together. We had each other. Our love for one another was epic at the peak of the terror, although we would each suffer the mental anguish no human should be made to carry, and would not wish upon another human . . . with the possible exception of Billy.

By the time we had gotten to the worst of the worst, we'd had to resign ourselves to so many terrible concessions that clinging to each other was all that was left. We saw Jean just slipping away forever, just out of reach, with no hope of a good outcome and knowing that she had no clue as to what was really happening to her, or to us. At this point, even the hunter/gatherer anger that was partially holding me up seemed a distant feeling.

I am really angry about a great many things regarding this situation. Just sitting here now, looking back three years at what we have been through, brings on a rush of emotions that makes my hands shake. If I had to compare it to a situation that most people have gone through, it feels like that exact moment in time when you suddenly realize you cannot not find your child in the crowd. It's terror, and that terror lasted every day, for months on end. Writing this brings it all back and the emotions well up again, as I remember it with complete clarity. There is a saying that goes: "Whatever doesn't kill you makes you stronger." I suppose for many everyday challenges that is a good way to justify going forward. But let me tell you, there are things that happen to people that beat them down and spit them out the other side in such a way that it does not make them stronger. It stays with them, it burdens them, and some never recover from the effects. We feel like we have aged ten years in the past three years. We are moving forward, but in a new direction. Even though our circumstance is a bit extreme, we want everyone to know what can happen and what they need to do to help protect themselves in normal circumstances of life. We want people to takes the five steps we outline in this book so that they can have the confidence and peace of mind that comes from being smart about their family and everything they have worked so hard for all of their lives.

I suppose there are many different decision paths that people choose at critical junctures in complicated, highly emotional life events. I found it best for me to zero in on "exactly what was the most important thing in all of this?" What is the one most important thing I would not want to risk in this whole new chapter of our lives? Within the question, the answer came: "Our lives."

Terrie and I have had an incredible life together. She is my "everything," and I am hers. Not in a dependent way, but as two who have lived their lives together in an encouraging and supportive way. We could not allow this situation to come between us. Terrie needed me to be there for her and I needed her to be there for me, just like we have always done, for better or for worse.

Besides, this was Terrie's mother. Even with all of our history and sense of shared families, I had no right to be an emotional steamroller or overbearing protector. Terrie was in the lead, and I would try my best to encourage, support, and love her. It wasn't always easy. Terrie and I discussed this at length. We melded together in our sorrow for Jean and pledged to find new strength through each other to make this transition in our lives with our heads held high.

CHAPTER 9

Jon

The advances in modern medicine are unbelievable. Throughout the entire hospitalization and aftermath of the wreck, we learned so much as we tried to fight for Jean's recovery.

The ability of doctors to diagnose and repair humans has grown on a scale that would have been unfathomable to doctors just a couple of decades ago. They could put Humpty Dumpty back together again these days. Planning for an extended life is more important than ever because of two factors: 1) medical advances enabling longer life; and 2) because of the medical advances, the chances of needing expensive long-term care have gone up significantly. Retirement has taken on a whole new aspect that many are not prepared for.

However, medical capabilities with the brain are still steeped in mystery. They know so much more, but the brain is so complex that when trauma has occurred the symptoms are far reaching and different for each person. The information given to families today about what to expect is still vague. The information given to us when we inquired about how to best care for a person with these injuries was vague, at very best. All they could tell us was what symptoms could occur and that it is different for for everybody, including: headache, confusion, change in behavior, dizziness, nausea and vomiting, lethargy or excessive drowsiness, weakness, apathy, and seizures. People may vary widely in their symptoms from a traumatic brain injury.

Besides the effects of a TBI, a person's age and other medical conditions can affect the overall response to the injury. So, in other words, they are not sure. For us, when we would ask for explanations of changes in behavior regarding Terrie's mom . . . well, we had already seen Jean become acutely obsessive about some things, like her calendar. She would walk around the house pointing at her day timer and mumbling to herself about what was on her schedule. Over and over and over, many times per day. Usually there was only one item per day on her schedule, but she struggled with getting the few items straight in her mind, which was extremely frustrating for her.

Looking back, we understand that we did everything we could to help her heal and give her the best care ever in the short time we were afforded. What's the lesson? Be prepared. Be as prepared as you can be for the unexpected. Because even though you think you know someone, all bets are off as they age, or have an injury, or get targeted by a predator. In our case it was all three at once, and these created a tornado of events we still cannot seem to get out of. Looking back now, we can evaluate each step we took, and we can see that we did the right things. The only thing we didn't do is prepare in advance for the worst-case scenario, because who imagines something like this would occur? We had prepared as best we could as a family.

We had all of the information we needed in case of a medical emergency. We are well versed in the family Trust and how to be good stewards of such a thing, and we are very communicative with our parents as well as our son. And not just communicative about all of the great things in life, but also regarding a possible uncertain future. So many people have not prepared and rely only on hope. They "hope" it will not happen to them or a loved one.

When it comes to anyone's future, only planning will save them and their family. That is why we are so passionate about sharing our story and offering solutions, because "hope" is not a plan. Even people with deep spiritual beliefs need to plan. You may have heard someone say, when someone dies prematurely, "God must have had a better plan for them." Well, what if your Higher Power—be it God, Allah, Buddha, The Universe, or whomever—has a "better plan" for you, your parents, your spouse, or your children? Are you prepared for that?

After the accident we were attentive, loving, and patient in hopes that Jean would fully recover. In fact, I'm not sure it ever occurred to us that she wouldn't. So in many ways, we felt blindsided by the turn of events.

Immediately following the accident, either Terrie or I would sit with Jean to go over what she was trying to do, but she would just get so angry with herself that we would have to try and get her to do something else to get her mind off of it. If she did seem to get it, we would praise her for trying, but then she would have whatever it was out just a few minutes later, going through the same process all over again.

Another obsession was her purse. She carried it with her everywhere: to the bathroom, watching television, at the dinner table, for short walks outside, everywhere. She would state, "Oh, I just like to have it close to me." If for some reason, which happened often, she would not be able to find her purse, or telephone, or some other item, she would go directly into high anxiety. Panic mode was over-the-top emotionally for her. She would try to backtrack when she last had whatever it was she had misplaced, but with the cognitive impairment she could not remember even a few minutes ago. Of course, we always held out hope this would change and that her brain function would be restored.

Then she would start making things up, like, "Maybe it's at my house" (even though she had not been to her house) or "I'm sure it's in my car" (even though she no longer had a car). We would have to immediately search for whatever lost item there was, and it would usually be close at hand and very visible. In her panic, she could not recognize the item even if it was in plain sight. She would be so obsessed with where she left the item that she would not see the item sitting right in front of her. One-dimensional thinking.

The best that doctors can do in this situation is to apply their super medical procedures and monitor signs that show improvement—or not. I believe that one of our mistakes was thinking that when the doctors said she would be fine, we thought she would be fine in all aspects. What the doctor meant was, "She is not going to die." With a TBI, they use the MRI tests to measure if the brain is expanding after the initial shrinkage from the trauma. They measure whether the injured brain is filling back into the space created by the trauma and how the patient is responding to manual cognitive testing.

When excess blood and fluids build up and surgery is needed, there are a few ways to approach the surgery.

Again, in my layman's explanation, the first is called a Burr Hole Trephination. A hole, or several holes, are drilled in the skull over the area of the subdural hematoma, and the blood is thinned and mixed around with treatment fluids, then suctioned out through the hole(s).

Next is the craniotomy. A larger section of the skull is removed to allow the doctors better visual access to the subdural hematoma and reduce pressure by removing blood and fluids. The removed skull is replaced shortly after the procedure.

Lastly is the craniectomy. A section of the skull is removed for an extended period of time to allow the injured brain to expand and swell without permanent damage. A Craniectomy is not often used to treat subdural hematoma unless the brain itself is overexpanding.

Every step of the way through the surgeries, medical professionals were compassionate and clear. Before surgery they explained potential outcomes. During, they communicated status, and after, the doctor said the surgery went very well and the Trephination surgery looked like it was working. They even explained that Jean would be in the intensive care unit so she could be monitored closely and that another MRI would be performed the following day. Throughout this process we held onto hope that her cognitive functions would be restored, and we'd have many more happy years with her.

After a week in the hospital, the doctor said that she could return home if she had supervision like before. I wished he had not told us that with Jean present, because what she heard was, "You can go to your own home now." She wasn't at all ready! But, she was an adult and she was strong willed.

Of course, that was not what the doctor meant, but that was a bone of contention between Jean and Terrie. We finally got Jean to understand that she would need to stay with us for a while longer so that we could keep a close eye on her condition and make sure she was comfortable. Looking back to that time, I recall how Jean's cognitive functions were still almost nonexistent. She had pretty good long-term memory from her early childhood, but she just had not improved much with any short-term memory function. She continued to carry her purse everywhere, and obsessed about her day timer, trying to understand what she had to do on certain days, but then not being able to remember any of it.

Another strange thing started to occur once we brought her home from the latest surgery. Whenever she would talk with Billy on the telephone, she would talk in a very overexuberant tone of voice. She would also tell him that she was doing so much better. She would have her day timer with her and would read what she had to do just like she was recalling this from memory.

We felt that she was afraid that he might break up with her due to her condition, and she was overcompensating in her mannerisms and voice inflection. Terrie and I discussed that she seemed to be acting like a little girl in these instances. Of course, there was nothing to do about this, and at least she seemed to be happy when she talked with Billy.

Billy seemed to be handling the new life of Jean OK. He was listening to Terrie, who was kind enough to keep him informed, and he also seemed resigned that everything was different now since the wreck and subsequent surgeries. I had thought that he would dump her like so much trash, but he continued to talk with Jean via telephone.

After a couple of weeks Terrie took Jean in to the doctor for a follow-up. Jean stated that she wanted to move back to her home. The doctor said he did not see a problem with that as long as she had someone with her. Jean did not understand why she needed anyone there, but the doctor said that she was still in a serious situation.

Jean stated that she was just fine, but the doctor pointed out that she still had to write down everything she wanted to talk about and had to read those notes every time. He told Terrie privately that people who have suffered a TBI often think they are much better than they are. Back at home, we discussed with Jean the need for someone to be with her, and that we would try to arrange something temporarily.

Terrie arranged for a couple of friends of Jean's to stay with her at her home for short periods during the day. This made

Jean feel better, and allowed us to catch up on some of our own lives that we had shelved to take care of her. During this time, I contacted the long-term care insurance people to find out what was permissible by their standards and to arrange in-home care. The insurance company sent a nurse out to visit with Jean and to test her cognitive abilities to make sure she met the company's requirements in order for them to pay for the in-home care. Jean met those standards very quickly during the testing.

I started contacting professional in-home care companies because these were the only options the long-term care insurance company would pay for. After sorting out which care companies were in the area and which ones seemed like they had good programs for care, we set up interviews with two of them. We met with the care manager at Jean's home with her in attendance. Of course, Jean was part of the decision process so that she could feel good about whoever was chosen, and we hoped this would avoid adding undue stress during this transition to her home.

We were amazed at how much in-home care costs were! For Jean to have a caretaker there with her for twelve hours a day came to approximately $9,000 per month. When I looked at different costs for care, I found that Welfare-qualified facilities ranged from about $3,000 to $5,000 per month. High-end full service care facilities were about $12,000 per month. We were certainly glad that Terrie went with her mother to buy long-term care insurance after her dad had died. I do not think many people think about this and would spend every penny they have should something catastrophic happen to them. People need to plan for this contingency as soon as possible.

After the in-home care company was selected, Terrie set up all of the business end with them and then started helping her mother adjust to being at home. We were both scared to death about this. Just a few weeks earlier Jean was in the ICU with tubes swirling liquid around her brain, and now she was moving back to her home.

I was proud of Terrie for the way she handled the transition back to her mom's house. Jean was scared, resisting the caregivers at first, claiming she was so uncomfortable having strangers in her home.

Terrie reassured her and reminded her that moving back to her house was what she wanted to do, and that it was going to take some time to find new routines. She continually expressed to Jean how nice it was going to be to have the caregivers helping her with the activities and academics she needed to get better at. This always seemed to buoy Jean's resolve . . . for that day anyway.

Terrie had one particular day that was very hard on her. Earlier in the day, she and I had gone to the cemetery to place Memorial Day flowers at the graves of her dad and brother. This trip to visit and pay respect for them was harder. With Jean being somewhat incapacitated, our hearts were so very heavy that morning. When we returned, Terrie went over to visit with her mom. During one of their conversations, Terrie mentioned that we had gone to the cemetery for Memorial Day. Terrie said that Jean didn't even bat an eye. It just did not register with her at all.

Prior to the accident, Jean would have had her flower arrangements all put together and would have gone to the cemetery with us or on her own. She did this for every birthday and Christmas too. Now, just to know what day it was, was a good day for Jean.

Terrie felt so badly that Jean had not even been able to relate to the subject of her late son and husband. It was another sign of just how severely injured Jean was. She was truly living in another world from the one Terrie had spent her entire life in, a heartbreaking realization for any child.

It was like watching a slow, agonizing death.

CHAPTER 10

Jon

Looking back now, I can see the signs we didn't see then that something was terribly wrong in Jean's personal life beyond just the brain injury. We were there every moment attending to her, visiting, helping, and checking up on her—and then the caregivers we hired were suddenly asking Terrie to cut back on calls and visits during certain parts of the day for a little while.

They said they felt it would help them to keep Jean on track with performing what used to be everyday routines and also with uninterrupted time doing book assignments to improve cognitive functions. This made sense and is the kind of guidance you would expect from a company that performs the services they do. Certainly focused routines would help Jean get better and also keep her away from the dark thoughts she was having about the new world she was living in and did not like.

A couple of days later, Terrie called her mom to see if she had tomorrow's appointment date written down. Jean couldn't remember, and had to check with the caregiver. Terrie received a call not long after she had spoken with her mom from the home care manager. The manager stated that Billy had called her asking about the appointment time because Mom was upset. She was confused and concerned as to why Jean or Billy didn't call Terrie to find that out because she was the point person for communications with the care company's management. Terrie told her she would call Billy tomorrow.

Of course, the hair stood up on the back of my neck at that news. Billy was not supposed to be interfering. But Terrie said she thought he was probably just thinking he was helping Jean and possibly did not understand how he might be hurting the process the caregivers were trying to help with Jean. Terrie said she would talk with him and make sure that he was going to re-direct Jean back to the caregivers should Jean come to him with a problem. He assured Terrie that he understood.

Now that Jean was in her own home adjusting to her new life, Terrie and I finally had some time to just be with each other. The roller coaster we had been riding for three nonstop months had taken us to new heights of tired, and in much need of some alone time to get a position fix on where we were in this nightmare and also to see where we were emotionally. It was so hard on us to have been thrust into this role, each of us in our own way. We were not sure of so many things; would Jean get better, and to what degree? Would the caregivers be able to help Jean calm down and find some semblance of routine? Were we making good decisions, and what decisions would we have to make tomorrow?

We decided it would be good to see a therapist to discuss the situation and what we were feeling. We had done this many years before for some other life adversity, and had found a wonderful woman named Deanna who we both felt a connection with. A tall, slender woman, physically fit from being active in rock climbing and other adventurous feats, Deanna had long, flowing black hair, and a welcoming demeanor in her movements and expressions. She had an easy way about her, and we were in need of someone in our life situation who had an "easy" way about them.

Terrie was feeling like she had lost the mother she had known all of her life without knowing if she would ever have that mother back again. Considering what we had seen, I would have said that would be unlikely. We benefited greatly from seeing Deanna, and she listened. It was great to hear that we were making the best decisions we could and that our open communication with each other was healthy and strong. She helped us understand the feelings we were having and gave us tools to better cope with these feelings. She also helped us to stay strong in our love and commitment to each other. We were trapped mentally, trying to reconcile something that was irreconcilable. Her professional techniques allowed us to be as understanding with this situation as possible.

We believe more people should get outside professional help with big life problems. It is a sign of strength and wisdom to want another informed, professional opinion of such things in life.

While editing this book during a week in August 2014, entertainer Robin Williams took his own life. The outpouring of grief as seen through the media, as well as social networks, had been intense. The positive conversations encouraging people to seek professional help for distressing thoughts and depression is a good thing, we believe.

When people are invoked in such a shock to the system, they tend to put their own life on the back burner, hoping things will get better. Although hope is a positive emotion, hope is not a plan. We must be intentional and forward-looking in our actions in order to help our hopes succeed.

When Jean moved back home and the caregivers took over, we took a few weeks to get our own work caught up. At Jean's house, though, the caregivers were encountering behaviors from Jean which had them quite concerned. She seemed more and more agitated about her situation and any little thing would just send her into a panic. Not being able to find her phone, or misunderstandings between her and the caregivers—anything.

They were also concerned for safety reasons. Jean had been found taking her daily medication twice one morning. She did not remember that she had taken them already. The caregiver manager, Marge, felt strongly that Jean should not be left alone due to the extreme memory problems. She did not want Jean to do something like leave the stove on or put herself in a precarious situation that might cause panic and not be able to remember how to get help, or not be able to get to safety. They decided to evaluate the situation daily over the next week, and Terrie wanted to talk with the doctor about this too.

Terrie was financial power of attorney for Jean, so she was paying her regular bills for her since the wreck. She met with Jean's financial advisor, to get her advice regarding Jean's funds. Now that she was receiving in-home care, there was uncertainty for a recovery in the time allotted for her to continue receiving care, even after her long-term insurance coverage expired. All of the females on Terrie's side of the family have lived well into their nineties, so having Jean's financial advisor look at her portfolio was critical in order to help ensure that her investments were situated in a way that continued to grow, but were also fairly liquid in case sudden substantial funds were needed.

Sherrie had been Jean's financial advisor for many years, and as Jean became older she always had Terrie at financial meetings with her in the event she did not totally remember something. Sherrie said that Terrie was doing a great job and that she would want to meet with Terrie and Jean to talk through the finances. Terrie set up that meeting with Jean and informed the caregivers.

Sherrie is a different type of financial advisor. Not just a numbers person, but someone who demonstrates a genuine caring for her customers. The type of professional who wants to know how you are doing personally, who remembers what was happening in your life the last time you met. She always has a smile on her face and is optimistic about her clients' well-being in all ways.

When Terrie and Sherrie met at Jean's house for that meeting, Jean was quite agitated. Looking back, I recall thinking it was probably normal. It hadn't really occurred to us there was anything seriously sinister going on behind the scenes in conversations between her and Billy, or anyone else.

Based on what we had observed recently, I felt sure that most of that nervous behavior was because it was going to be a meeting, talking about many things, and Jean was probably concerned about keeping up with the conversation and getting everything right in her mind. When they started, Jean pulled out some notes she had made and dove right in, starting by asking questions. She really did not understand what she was talking about, but doggone it, she was going to show that she was in charge! And this was the meeting we mentioned earlier, where Jean got focused in on a check for $12,000 that went out. Sherrie explained to her that this was the check that paid for last year's tax debt.

Jean kept coming back to that check over and over, sometimes writing the same notes that she had already written. Sherrie went through everything with them and made some suggestions toward future adjustments if needed. She said that with so much up in the air, she felt it best to just keep a close eye on how things developed with Jean before making any decisions now.

After that meeting, Sherrie called Terrie and said, "Oh my gosh, Terrie, she's getting worse." Terrie told her that she didn't think that she was getting worse, but that her mom was fighting for freedom and did everything she could to give the appearance of how well she was when it mattered.

Terrie also told Sherrie that when Jean had anxiety or obsessed about something, such as her finances, then she did get really confused and agitated. Sherrie said that she felt so bad about this—for Mom and us. She said that because of the difficulties in working with the bank with power of attorney, Jean really needed to put Terrie on the checking account too. Sherrie had seen this before with clients and said that if Jean didn't decide to put her on the checking account in the next week, that she thought Terrie would need to start the guardianship process right away. Terrie questioned that, and Sherrie reiterated that she felt very strongly about it. Sherrie said, "She's going to be mad at you, but it needs to happen." Looking back now, my wife only put her mother's emotions first.

Should we have treated it all differently?

Probably yes, but in extreme situations, second guessing decisions can be just as dangerous as jumping in too soon. Terrie was acting in the best interest of her mother, and giving her the benefit of the doubt, just as we would want if it were us.

Terrie and I talked at length about the finances, and ultimately we decided to wait a while longer before doing something that would certainly add more stress to Jean. Terrie wanted Jean to at least get to a point where she was working better with the caregivers, and then she would reassess the guardianship question.

In hindsight, I see another bend in the road that should have raised big red flags.

On one particular day I called the caregiver office because we hadn't received a bill from them yet. I found out that they'd mailed out two, both to Jean's address. I had that changed to our address. I called Marge to ask if she'd have the caregivers watch for bills and then put them in the caregiver's report book so I could get them there. It was then that Marge said that the caregivers had a concern about Billy.

Two of them had called Marge to say that they were concerned that Jean was getting sidetracked and not wanting to focus on her brain exercises. They also said that Billy had told them to document the phone calls that Jean received from family. One of the caregivers, Claudia, had called Marge to say that Billy was there that morning and that the three of them were leaving and she didn't know when they'd be back.

I received a call from Sue at the injury attorney's office. She told me that Jean had called the car insurance company that morning to find out when she'd be getting a check for the car. Sue arranged that I would receive the check for the vehicle so that it could be deposited into Jean's account.

I called Jack, the personal injury attorney, to let him know about the Billy visit and subsequent phone call to her car insurance company. He suggested that he meet Jean by himself the next week to start to develop a rapport with her. Terrie also called Dr. Fields's office to make arrangements to have Mom see this specialist. The receptionist said Terrie should hear back from her in a week as to whether she'd received all the records from the hospitals that she needed.

Terrie had called Jean and left a message to put another appointment on her calendar. Later, the caregiver and Terrie spoke on the phone. She said that she was really having challenges with Jean and her obsession over Billy.

TERRIE

She said that they would have to drop everything at any time Billy called to go to him, or if he came over to see Jean he was the only priority. The caregiver said that she couldn't keep driving Jean to far-away places for breakfast, as she didn't have a dependable car and didn't want to put that much wear on the car she did have. She said that Jean needed more structure and the caregivers were frustrated because there was no food in the house and all Jean wanted to think about was going somewhere with Billy.

I asked her to call Marge and express her concerns, and then have Marge call me, and at that point we would call Billy. Claudia said, "You're doing the right thing, Terrie. Your Mom is not OK". I thanked her for the support and for the great job they were doing.

JON

We went over to Jean's to visit her and talk with the caregivers about some of the frustrations they were feeling. While there, I noticed that there was a state driving manual on the kitchen table. I showed Terrie and she asked the caregiver what the manual was for. The caregiver said that Billy had gotten that for Jean so she could take the driving test and get her license back.

I pulled Terrie aside and let her know that he had crossed the line and that something needed to be done about Billy. Terrie and I talked at length about him, and about his inability to be a part of the healing process with Jean. I urged Terrie to be more firm with him on the call she was going to make to him. She agreed, but things took a turn for the worse before that call could be placed.

JUNE 30

Terrie called me at work and told me that one of the caregivers had called her and was very concerned about Jean, who was experiencing blurry vision, unsteadiness, and extreme confusion. They were worried it was a possible stroke. They were at Billy's house. Terrie said she had told the caregiver to take her mom to the Providence Hospital emergency room. I left work immediately, picked up Terrie at our house, and drove straight to the hospital.

When we arrived at the hospital and went in to the lobby, Billy was sleeping on one of the benches in the waiting room. I thought, "Well there is a caring, worried man." We went in to see how Jean was. She was very confused and could hardly talk to answer the doctors' questions. Claudia, the caregiver, was there too. A psychologist came in and asked us to leave so that she could talk with Jean alone. Terrie, Claudia, and I went into another room close by. Claudia talked of how Billy was not being helpful and was always telling Jean he didn't think anything was wrong with her and that everyone was just overreacting. Claudia seemed very, very concerned for Jean. The doctor prescribed something for Jean that would help with the anxiety, but Terrie wanted to call Dr. Nguyen first to see if it was OK to combine with the other medications she was taking.

After the psychologist had finished with Jean, she came in and spoke with us. After that conversation, we talked with Jean for a bit to make sure she was well enough to leave the hospital. As we were leaving, I noticed that Billy was no longer in the waiting room. I asked the front desk nurse if he had left a message, and she said that he had said he was going to the car to sleep because it was too noisy. Terrie asked me if I thought she should call and have the talk with him and I said yes.

Terrie called his number twice, but no answer. I was ready to have my own talk with him at that point, and went to the parking lot to try and find him. I looked through the parking lot but couldn't locate him, so we all left in our car and returned Jean to her house. Claudia made plans to go get her car at Billy's house with one of the other caregivers. Jean went to bed, and we thanked Claudia for calling when she noticed there was something wrong.

When Terrie and I arrived back at our house, I was pretty upset at what Billy was doing and the anguish he was causing. I had spoken to the accident attorney earlier, but decided I needed to relay to him what the current situation was. He wasn't available by telephone, so I decided to write him an email:

Hi Jack,

Jean did not have a stroke.

She is so worried that everybody is 'out to get her' constantly, according to one of the caretakers, that apparently her blood pressure rose to a point that caused stroke symptoms. The caretaker revealed that Jean had spoken about suicide twice yesterday. The social worker at the emergency room said that she did not feel Jean was a high threat for that after speaking with her, but did strongly feel that she needs psychological help. She also recommended Terrie get help to navigate through this lose/lose situation. We have not heard from Providence regarding their approval of Dr. Fields yet. The emergency room prescribed Xanax to try and take the edge off of her depression and anxiety. Terrie is going to check with Dr. Nguyen (Neurosurgeon) this morning to see if he is okay with Jean taking the medicine before filling the prescription. We also found out yesterday that Billy has given Jean the DMV book to study for getting her driver license back.

The social worker yesterday said that this was concerning because, on her own, Jean would not be able to accomplish this. No one caring for her would allow her to do that at this time, but with Billy in the picture, she has a way to actually get there to attempt the test. She also said that with Billy aiding Jean as if nothing is really wrong with her, opens the door for a whole host of detrimental possibilities. The care company manager is going to call Billy this morning to ask him not to call Jean between 9 am and noon, so that Jean can focus on her cognitive exercises without worrying if he is going to call.

The care workers have expressed concern to their Man-

ager of driving Jean several times a week to Billy's home in West Linn, or to Estacada for breakfast with Billy. They definitely feel he is detrimental to their efforts and Jean's recovery. Terrie is going to see if there is anything she can do through the care company rules to minimize these drives.

Jack, Billy is whacked, and although I am usually calm and dependable in times of crisis, I find my patience wearing very thin because of what this is doing to my wife and how his actions are making Jean's condition worse. Not sure what that means, other than venting that my hunter/gatherer, 32-years-of-marriage self is really pissed. Nobody on our professional team seems to have the authority or inclination to do anything about his actions, which compounds my feelings.

After today's events, Terrie is resolved to pursue guardianship, but is heeding your request to meet with Jean next Tuesday. I believe Terrie is going to call Matt today regarding this action. I agree with her assessment that this move is necessary to protect Jean from herself, hold Billy and/or other third party distractions accountable to what is best for Jean, and to ensure that Jean has the best care and help she needs to hopefully recover.

Regards,
Jon Hull

I did not hear back from Jack that afternoon, but he did call the next day. I reiterated our concerns, but Jack said, "Well, I wouldn't worry about that right now until I can talk with Jean."

CHAPTER 11

Enough is Enough

We were mind-boggled. There are so many others who have been through their own horrible circumstances of life, on the treadmill of coping with everything all at once, while under great stress.

Although Terrie and I have been through adversities, this one kicked us right in the gut day in and day out. It has been all that we can do some days to keep our emotions together with the horrible situation Jean was, and still is, in. Perhaps it was because we were powerless to help, give love, or comfort her as much now that she was at her home and the caregivers were asking for more space to work with Jean. At the same time, I saw the joy in my wife slipping away.

When I met Terrie all those years ago in high school, she was a ball of fire. Good grades, playing lead roles in the theater, singing with the swing and concert choirs, as well as violin with the orchestra. She had a lot of energy too. We had a couple of classes together our sophomore year and one day we noticed each other. Terrie is as true blue a soul as there can be. She is of the highest integrity of anyone I have ever met, and she exudes her Midwestern roots through her incredible cooking, pleasant demeanor, belief in family-first values, and work-hard ethics. As a professional, she is the person you would want to have helping you no matter what it was you were buying. You would leave thinking, *I wish everyone was like that.*

After high school, she earned her radio broadcasting degree and spent the next eighteen years in the radio industry before moving into executive leadership roles. She is now a successful business owner of two service-oriented businesses.

To know Terrie is a blessing. She makes me want to strive to be a better person, a better husband, a better father, a better professional, a better man. We have both worked for more fulfillments in our lives, and each of us has supported and encouraged that growth for each other. As change has come more quickly through the generations, we have each allowed space for each other to change with the times. Obviously, after so many years together, there is a sense of oneness. Our likes are similar in almost every fashion of our lives. We are beyond best friends; we are connected at the soul until death do we part. A friend of ours once remarked, "You grew up like twins."

Looking back at the adversity we have faced, I'm glad to hang on to the fact that the best part of it, the silver lining, is that we have bonded together more intensely than ever. What doesn't kill you makes you stronger, right?

The morning after the hospital incident with Jean, Terrie and I discussed Billy's apparent control with Jean. He had now stepped over the line by getting her the driving manual. He was promising her something she would not succeed at. He was filling her with unrealistic stories of being normal again and trying to convince her that he was the only one who could help her. It was confusing—we didn't believe she could do it because we'd known her before the accident and could see the impairment. We were also extremely concerned for the lives of other drivers on the road.

That was probably the breaking point. That was the moment that Terrie and I determined that it was time to lawyer up and see what we could do to stop Billy from interfering any further. This was not a difficult decision based on what was happening, but we knew that it would mean Jean would have to also deal with Billy being out of the picture. We knew this would be very, very difficult for her, but allowing Billy to continue being an obstacle in her rehabilitation was not healthy for any of us, and could cause a great deal of damage to her long-term mental health. I started making some calls, but with it being the Friday before the Fourth of July weekend, not many people were available. We were so looking forward to the weekend, as it was the first time since the wreck that we had an opportunity to go out of town for a few days by ourselves.

LATER THAT MORNING

Terrie needed to call her mom that morning because she wanted to talk with the caregivers to see how Jean was doing after the previous day. She also needed to stop by to have her sign papers for direct deposit for the long-term care insurance benefits and to authorize a copy of her car title for the DMV.

While I was at work that morning, Terrie called me in a panic. She said that when she called over to her mom's, a police officer answered the phone and told her that there was a situation there. And that's when the sudden severity of the situation crystallized. It was the moment when our lives would change forever, when reality would shift into a macabre journey that would test our strength, love, and sanity.

Officer Powers said that Jean and Billy were accusing Terrie of stealing large sums of money from her mother's accounts. Terrie said that she had explained to Officer Powers what had happened to her mom in the wreck, what her mental state was, and what Billy had been doing. She told the officer to check the facts and ask for proof of the assertions which Billy was claiming. However, Officer Powers decided on her own that she was going to take Terrie to task rather than investigate Terrie's side of the story.

Officer Powers became judge and jury. Terrie argued the point, but the officer said that Terrie was just like Officer Powers' two family members, fighting over their mother's money.

I was stunned. My mind was spinning as Terrie was relaying this new turn of events. I had never heard Terrie so upset. She could not comprehend Officer Powers's stance of "knowing" her mom. It turns out that Officer Powers had given Jean three traffic citations several months before the wreck for not completely stopping at a stop sign that she regularly staked out. Jean had been very worried about losing her license, and Terrie had worked with Jean diligently about her driving habits after those tickets.

So now Officer Powers "knew" Jean and decided that Terrie was lying about the money. She wanted Terrie to turn over all of the ledgers she had been keeping for her mother's finances, without any proof from Jean or Billy of the purported theft.

We would learn later that Officer Powers had previously been in hot water for being a bully rather than a public servant. Apparently, several years prior, Officer Powers had come across a disabled homeless woman who was living in her car. This poor woman was given three citations for a concealed weapon (brass knuckles), driving with a suspended license, and driving without insurance. Officer Powers had the car towed away, leaving this woman out on the street and owing hundreds of dollars just to get her car back. The charges were all dropped by the city.

This is an officer who was supposed to be working for the welfare of the people, but from what we experienced, her methods were personally motivated by utilizing a hunch and a badge.

I believe that everyone has an expectation that when dealing with a public servant in any capacity, these professionals will be acutely aware of their responsibilities and conduct themselves in the highest professional manner. But in this case, Officer Powers was making her own spin on the events at hand and was going to make sure Terrie was held accountable for the "theft" that never happened. Officer Powers was not only going to be judge and jury, but also executioner. Officer Powers gave Terrie until the Tuesday following the holiday weekend to turn over the ledger.

We tried to reach attorney Todd Meek. Mr. Meek was the elder law attorney we had spoken to after the wreck to see what we needed to do in that situation and find out if we were being proper in how we were handling Jean's situation so far. At that time, Mr. Meek had said we were doing everything by the book and to check back with him should the situation change. Due to the holiday weekend, he was not in his office.

We decided that we needed to get away from the house in case Officer Powers wanted to insert herself further into our lives, plus we needed to think about what was going on and to reach some of Jean's professional team to alert them of this kidnapping.

Apparently, Billy had seen that Jean was slipping away from him during the hospital incident. So he made his move by lying to the police. He was going to get his way by hook or by crook. The problem before us was how to stop Billy from doing just that now that he had the police doing his bidding for him.

We went to the family cabin that night. It was a quiet ride as we both could not understand how Officer Powers could be so negligent in her duties, or how Jean could possibly go along with Billy in bringing charges up against Terrie. The obvious answer to the latter was that Jean had been unduly influenced by Billy. Yes, he was so deranged in his thinking that he would influence a brain-injured woman into thinking that the only daughter she had, in fact the only direct relative she had, besides her brother in Texas, had stolen money from her. The weekend at the cabin was one of tears, fears, and anger.

We were able to get through to Jean's financial planner, Sherrie, to let her know what was happening. We also contacted Jean's estate attorney, Bill Best, to inform him of what Billy had done. Bill said that he would try to contact Jean to get a take on the situation. He also said he would not allow Billy to change anything in her estate plan.

Later that day, Sherrie called and said that Jean had just called her to inform her that she was closing all of her investment accounts and moving them to another firm. Sherrie was beside herself. She knew that Billy was orchestrating this, but there was nothing she could do except try and stall the transfer process. She said she could only stall for a couple of days, so we needed to take some type of action as soon as possible.

Terrie's Uncle Dave was also very upset at the news. Later that same day, Dave called Terrie and said that Billy had called him to say that Terrie was stealing money and wanted to put Jean in a home. He said he told Billy that Terrie would never do such a thing. He also told Billy never to contact him again. Dave said that he was going to contact other family members around the country to warn them of a possible call from Billy and what was happening with Jean.

As we sorted through all of these details, it amazed me how each detail came back in vivid color. I suppose writing this book is therapeutic, because in some way we know we will help others see themselves in our lives. Hopefully, if you read something and recognize red flags, you'll be able to step in and take precautions. Before the worst happens, take steps to prepare and protect you and your family.

It was the morning after the 4th of July, and we were on the road early heading back to town. We were resolved to get ahold of Todd to see what course of action we needed to be taking. At 9 a.m. we stopped in the middle of the desert to give Todd a call. He was not in, but his office manager transferred me directly to his cell phone. I explained to Todd what had transpired to date and asked him what we should do. He said that it looked as if we were going to have to go through the court system in order to get this resolved. I asked him if he saw this type of situation very much, and he said that this was not new, but it was most always the children who were trying to steal the money, not the boyfriend.

I asked Todd what we should do in the meantime. He said that we really needed to get ahold of Matt first so that we were covered from that end. I was starting to feel annoyed and helpless that something couldn't be done sooner.

"Todd, there has to be something we can do today!" Todd said that we could go to Elder Protection Services in town and file a complaint with them and that he felt pretty certain that any attorney representing us would have us do that. Feeling a little better, I thanked him and we continued on our way back to town.

When we arrived home, we gathered the documentation Terrie had been keeping about Jean, the paperwork the accident attorney said she needed so he could present this in the lawsuit he had filed against the driver that ran into her. We took that information and headed to the offices of Elder Protective Services. We met with one of the case workers, who took our statement and copied the documentation for his records. There were a few times when the case worker said, "Grimes [Jean's last name], Grimes . . . where have I heard that name before?" He would just look at us after each time he said this. As we would find out later, Billy had taken Jean here and they filed a claim against Terrie the day he made his move on Jean. We have wondered if Officer Powers guided Billy through that process too.

On the way home from Elder Protective Services, we received a call from Todd. He said that he had reached Matt Downs, who was a leading elder law attorney in town. He said that he had discussed the situation with him and Matt had agreed to meet with us to discuss the case further. We called Matt and he briefly went over what Mr. Meek had told him. He basically had the gist of it, and we set an appointment with him for first thing the next morning. Terrie explained what Officer Powers had said and done, and Matt said he knew Officer Powers and he was not surprised by her actions.

We met with Matt at his office. Matt explained that he was an elder law attorney, but that he always represented the elderly person in cases where the children were up to no good. He said that under the circumstances, he would take our case because it was so convoluted and there were gray areas in the state's elder laws that he understood well and was ready to face. We told him that Officer Powers would be wanting the ledger, and Matt said to let him talk with Officer Powers to see if he could just get her to look at the facts we were stating to her about Jean's medical condition and Billy's apparent motives.

Matt called us later in the evening and said he had talked to Officer Powers and that she was going to hold off on contacting us until he could look further into the situation. It was a relief to finally have someone fighting in our corner. We thanked him profusely and agreed to talk with him the next day. Terrie and I held each other tight the entire evening. What an exhausting past few days it had been! Just when we thought we were on a good track with helping Jean, the world exploded around us. Sleep was out of the question, eating was too, and the fear for Jean's well-being and the loathing for Billy were nearly unbearable.

CHAPTER 12

Protect and Serve

We awoke the next morning and started to get ready for the day. We had a meeting with Matt set for late morning and we both had to make the necessary arrangements for our jobs to free ourselves up. At 7 a.m., there was a knock on the door. I looked out of the window and there was a police car parked in front and Officer Powers was approaching the door. Terrie exclaimed to me that she thought Officer Powers was going to hold off until we had spoken with Matt again, but here she was knocking on our door. We were both still in our bathrobes, but I answered the door. This was the first time I had met Officer Powers face to face. She was standing just off of the front porch and she was facing the ground for some reason, holding out some papers that were rolled up in her hand. She said, "These are for you" without looking up.

I said, "I'm sorry, you are . . . ?" She looked up, surprised to see me standing there rather than Terrie. She said, "I need to give these to Terrie." I asked her what they were. She said, "Oh, just some paperwork for your wife." I said, "We were told that you were not going to bother us until we met with our attorney today." She said, "Well, I just needed to drop off these papers."

Terrie came to the door and asked Officer Powers, "What are those papers?" Officer Powers said, "This is a restraining order. You are not to try and contact your mother at all until this is cleared up."

Well, this was a new wrinkle, but here we were, Officer Powers doing things her way again. Fortunately, we were savvy enough through our work with attorneys during our leadership years to know what to do. I turned to Terrie and said, "She needs to serve those to Matt."

Terrie stated to Officer Powers that she needed to serve the papers to our attorney. Officer Powers said, "Well I'm here, so just take them now."

Terrie said, "I have asked you to serve those papers to our attorney."

Officer Powers then just laid the papers on the porch in front of me and said, "I am just going to consider these served and leave them here."

I said, in a not-so-polite tone, "Look, Officer Powers, you have been instructed to serve those to our attorney; what part of that do you not understand?"

Officer Powers started to walk off and then turned around and came back to the porch and picked up the papers. She asked, "So who is your attorney?" I said, "Matt Downs, you know that, you just talked with him last night." Officer Powers asked, "I don't have his number, do you have it?" I said, "You just talked to him last night; the number is still in your phone."

Officer Powers pulled out her cell phone and started scrolling. She said, "I don't seem to have that anymore, could you get me the number?" Terrie said she would get the number and left the room.

Officer Powers was fumbling with her phone as if she was trying to find the number, but I could tell she was taking pictures of me, in my bathrobe. No telling what she was going to use those pictures for. Terrie brought the number and handed it to her. I slammed the door shut and went to call Matt and leave him a message as to what just transpired. Now I had seen Officer Powers at work, and I knew why Terrie was so distrustful of her . . . a real piece of work, as they say.

We met with Matt late in the morning and told him what had transpired with Officer Powers earlier. Matt was beside himself that she had done this when she had told him that she would hold off. He said that Officer Powers was sure that Terrie had stolen money from Jean and was taking action based on her "gut feeling." Terrie went over all of the financials with Matt and he said that clearly Terrie had not done anything wrong and all the funds were accounted for.

Matt called Elder Protective Services, but they said that they had not received any financials from Jean or Officer Powers. Matt relayed what he had found in going over Terrie's financial records for Jean, and he sent those documents over to them to review. Matt had obtained the restraining orders filed by Jean and Billy as well.

CHAPTER 13

Gone, Gone

What happens when the unexpected happens to you?

When we finally saw the restraining order court documents, we saw that Billy had stated that Terrie was stealing $20,000 a month from Jean, while Jean stated on her form that Terrie had taken $30,000 so far. In reviewing Jean's filing, she did not spell Terrie's name correctly, did not know her age, did not describe her car properly, said that Terrie was driving by her house several times a day, could not give our home address, and both Jean and Billy said they were afraid of me because I owned a gun.

Officer Powers must have run a check on me to find that out and conveyed that information to Billy, because they would not have known that otherwise. Again, allegations with no proof. I would certainly need to look in to how they could get the restraining orders approved through the courts with absolutely no proof of what they were alleging.

Later that afternoon, Terrie received the call from Jean telling her that she and Billy had gotten married, and it was at this point that I knew nothing would be the same and Jean was gone, gone. Gone because of the severely debilitated state of mind her injuries had left her in, and gone because Billy had made the ultimate move to steal her away forever.

Devastated does not even come close to how we were feeling at that moment in time. Everything had happened so fast, and under the watchful eyes of Officer Powers, and apparently the courts. We were terrified. Trying to reconcile the events in our minds was impossible for us.

As you go through the motions of protecting your own family, please let us guide you based on our expertise and unfortunate experience. What you see now may not be what things look like in the future. When money is involved, the neighbors, friends, partners, or allies you think you have may turn on you. We had no idea about the predator lurking in the bushes. We were ambushed, in fact, many places along the way.

I obtained the court audio recording of when the restraining orders were brought before the judge. The judge read aloud from the papers which had been submitted. Then, there was Claudia's voice! Yes, the caregiver who had been working so closely with Terrie. The caregiver who had been sounding additional alarms about Billy. The caregiver who was with us at the hospital telling us how confused Jean was and that Billy was the cause of Jean's distress. There she was, telling the judge exactly what was written on the complaint forms. We would find out later that Claudia had actually helped Billy and Jean write up the complaint forms. What a shock!

After Claudia spoke to the judge, the judge called Jean forward. The judge asked, "So let's hear what proof there is."

She asked Jean to explain the the situation where, they claimed, we had taken her and Claudia away from the hospital against their will. I could not believe what I was hearing! Apparently they had contrived a story that they wanted Billy to take them home from the hospital after Jean's breakdown the previous week. Jean started to mumble a bit, obviously not remembering what Billy and Claudia had told her to say.

Jean then said, "I was in an accident and I have a hard time remembering." The judge said, "Oh, why don't you tell me about that." Jean said, "Well I really don't remember much about that either."

The judge asked who else she had with her and Jean said, "Well, Billy is here, we just got married!" The judge became so happy for her and congratulated them on the marriage.

The judge asked Billy what proof he had. Billy said, "They want to put her in a home and take all of her money." The judge said, "Oh, well let's put that in here too." The judge was apparently writing and said that she would approve the restraining orders. The judge also said that she was glad Claudia had been there and that Jean was lucky to have her along. Unbelievable!

The justice system has checks and balances to make sure things are what they appear to be, and to garner the proof needed to determine the course of action. But here they were, a rogue police officer acting on a gut feeling without a shred of proof, and a court judge approving two restraining orders, again without a shred of proof offered. And not only that, the judge made that decision after hearing that there was an accident involving Jean that made it nearly impossible for her to remember anything, and her brand new husband just stating what he wanted the judge to believe, again, without a shred of proof. In addition, the judge was looking at two orders which were claiming differing amounts of money taken. You would think that bells and whistles would be ringing the alarm for her to look into this further. Then, to top it off, Claudia aiding and abetting Billy in this whole elaborate scheme. The caregiver had now become the caretaker!

The justice system had just failed us and Jean, both.

Billy, the fox, was handed the keys to the chicken coop without any proof offered. Proof, the one thing that Officer Powers and the judge needed in order to proceed, in order to fulfill their job responsibilities as officials representing justice as public servants. In one mind-blurring week the world had changed forever for us. All of the traditions of our family, the love, the history, the shared good and bad of a lifetime together, still alive in our minds but . . . at the same time, it was all shattered beyond recognition.

We met with Matt to go over everything and find out what our course of action was going to be. He said that the restraining orders had to be cleared through the courts first and then we could file for a third-party conservator to take care of Jean's money—if there's anything left. I asked him why there was nothing in place that would allow someone in authority to just undo the restraining orders since there was no proof. He said that there should be, but we were now stuck in the court system and the only way to get the restraining orders vacated was to request a hearing and present the evidence. For that, we would have to wait another three weeks for a hearing.

Three weeks! Billy just stole Jean based on allegations and now the justice system was going to give him another three weeks to do as he pleased with Jean and her money. Matt also said that getting a court date for the conservator request would probably take four to six months. Well, that pretty much sealed the deal for Billy. It was heartbreaking to listen to.

The "good" news didn't stop there. Matt said that the marriage really screwed things up for us. It gave Billy certain legal rights as a husband, like being able to do business for Jean and pretty much do as he pleased with her money, unless Jean did something about that on her own. He also told us that in our State, once someone remarries, any will that may have been in place is voided. Matt was so very upset and sorry for us. Terrie and I were both in tears at this point. I reached over and put my hand on her shoulder. When she looked at me, I could see pain that I had never seen in my dear bride's eyes. I can't remember the rest of the day after that. I think my mind had reached the point where I could not bear this reality anymore, and it just shut me down.

CHAPTER 14

For Better or Worse

*"A good marriage is each for the other
and two against the world."*

—DAVE BRAULT

Marriage is for richer or poorer, for better or worse.

We were able to find out later some details regarding "the marriage" from the ADL sheets which the caretakers filled out each day. They would write down what activities and cognitive function therapies Jean performed that day along with notes of good and bad things Jean had demonstrated.

Interesting that Claudia did not turn in an ADL for the day she was in court lying to a judge. Anyway, on the day they were married, Billy had prearranged for one of the caretakers (one that we had never heard of) to wake Jean and help her get ready for a trip. That morning Billy, Jean, and the caretaker flew to Las Vegas and the two were married. They stayed the night and flew back the next morning. Billy never did buy her a ring. I imagine Billy must have thought this was great! Get married and then leave Jean with the caretaker while he was out on the town. What a party! Billy had everyone doing his bidding, and obviously Jean was saying yes to everything because she only knew what Billy was telling her. Before the wreck, Jean would never have married again in a thousand years. She had her independence, good friends, no concern for finances, and she had loved Terrie's dad so much it just wouldn't be something she would have done.

In fact, Jean had told Terrie that if she ever changed her mind about marriage, she would certainly get a prenuptial agreement after what had happened to Terrie's grandfather (Jean's father). You see, when Jean was about fifty, her father remarried. His wife seemed like a nice enough lady, but one day Jean received a call from banker in North Dakota saying that the wife was having papers finalized transferring all of his bank accounts over to her! Jean was so angry about that that she fought that process hard and thwarted the attempt. It was certainly nice that someone called Jean to warn her, someone going above and beyond their job.

They sometimes still do those things in small towns, because that's what you do when you are honest and care about what is right.

Organizing one's emergency information, as well as preparing a will and trust, appointing a power of attorney, and making medical directive is the responsibility of every parent, in our opinion. The problem these days is that most people don't do any of these. As best we can tell, there are those who have done this for generations as trusts, information, and stories are passed along family lines, and the hows and whys are explained to the children at the appropriate time so they can follow along and take responsibility when the time comes.

Then there are those who do not do it at all. It would seem there can be many reasons for this; maybe they grew up in a family that did not pass along the critical need to do it, and since it is not taught in school, how would they know but for a happenstance or from someone else, like us? The reasons and excuses are widely varied.

The facts are it is one of the most caring and forward-looking things one can do for their family. Without these, a family is faced with many obstacles, some of which will never be accomplished because they don't have the information needed to move forward. This will add immeasurable stress to family at a time when they are already having major stress in their lives. I think it is important to briefly go over these items here. Of course this is just in layman's terms.

1) ORGANIZING EMERGENCY INFORMATION

When Jean was involved in the car wreck, we had all of Jean's information, and thought we were prepared. We were able to jump into action because of this. We were able to call everyone on her professional team and put everything needed into motion with her insurances. Without organizing your information and assigning power of attorney, how can you expect your spouse or child to know what they don't know? How will they know about the storage rental you have? How will they know the computer passwords needed to handle those affairs? How will they know who your lawyer(s), doctors, insurance agents, or financial advisors are? What about your company? Who is going to take care of these same things for them? Having these things organized, in one place for easy access, is critical. Having a durable power of attorney assigned will give that person the legal right to access and handle the disposition of everything, if you assign everything. From our life experiences we can assure you that without such safeguards, you will be putting more on their plate than they think they may be able to handle at a time when they are not at their best to handle things like this at all.

2) WILLS AND TRUSTS

After you have organized everything and determined what your wishes are should something happen, this is when you will need to seek out a great estate attorney and have these documents drawn up. The key is to have your plan of action ready so the attorney can put everything in the proper order the way you want. These documents and their use will vary greatly depending on your wishes, circumstances, and assets. A great attorney will know if you need both. Don't get stuck on not knowing how these work. The best advice we can give is to keep it as simple as possible! Convoluted estate plans can be a mess for your family. Wording should be clear so no one can say, did you mean this, or that.

3) POWER OF ATTORNEY

Depending on the laws in your state, designating a Durable Power of Attorney for financial and medical decisions gives your designee(s) the legal right to help you. Without this, a family member will have to go through the court system to have, possibly, a third party of the court system take care of everything for your family at another cost, along with the courts and lawyers taking a slice of your family's financial pie. You don't have to have a lawyer to do this, although it is advisable. Just assign everything and have it notarized. Medical and financial don't cover everything though; items like pass-words to personal accounts are just one of many items you want to detail. Insist that your attorney includes specific access to everything so your designee does not run into a specific entity which says, your power of attorney does not specifically state you grant you access to the safe deposit box. This is just one example of course and there are too many to list here. If your attorney does not have POA forms for digital assets, or says you don't need that, we would question how current their practice of law is.

4) ADVANCE MEDICAL DIRECTIVE

Having a medical directive in place takes away a decision that nobody should ever have to make for you. The terror family members can endure by having to be the one to decide an end of life situation is unfathomable. I remember when Terrie's dad was dying and he did not have a directive. Jean was so distraught with having to make that decision. It stayed with her forever after that. Please do not put anyone in that position.

As you have read, or perhaps experienced, having the legal system involved with your family's personal business is a worst-case scenario. Families are torn apart every day because of this. Emotions are already running high and now they need to try and figure out all of this? Dissension can build when they reach the point where they can't deal with it. Don't let the courts decide what will happen to your assets and money. They don't care about you or your family, it is merely a process for them, and as you have read they might just mess it up!

It's also important to understand that these things cannot be done once it's too late, ever! Please do not procrastinate unless you can tell your family the exact day that you will be in a car wreck, or have a workplace accident, or contract a deadly disease, or just not wake up. Take total control of something you have total control of for the sake of those you love. Give them the legal right.

There is a rule in law—it's not a law, just a rule of thumb—*"If it's not in writing, it didn't happen."* You may have told someone what you wanted to have happen, but the court only recognizes legally binding documents. If there is one thing you take away from this book, make it that statement. Without everything in place and in official writing, anyone can say, "It never happened."

We were recently giving a talk on this subject to a group, and a woman made a statement that really shined a light on this statement. She exclaimed, "If something ever happened to me and my husband, we know who we want to take care of our children." I asked, "Do you have that in writing, and included in your official documents?" Everyone could see the terror wash over her. I explained that without that provision in your documents, your friend has no legal right to do anything. Your intent has not been made legally official. Your friend can request that she be the one to take care of them, but she will be requesting that of the state's Human Services Department—you know, the government. They may decide otherwise and she will be helpless to convince them otherwise. If your intent has been made clear regarding your children, your friend at least has legal ground to fight from. She will still have to jump through the hoops the government has outlined for her to be a good fit to care for your children, but they cannot just make that decision in a vacuum. Fortunately, Terrie's family had a will and a trust.

Once the will was voided by the new marriage, the trust still gave Terrie the legal right to fight for a conservator. It also gave Matt a fighting chance in the case, because the trust showed the intent that her parents had in regards to how they wanted their assets and finances to be handled. This is very important; without the trust in Terrie's family, we would have been done, toast, finished after Billy sprang his grand scheme. Terrie would not have had the high legal ground to pursue a fight for a conservator; it would have been her word against Billy's, with Jean agreeing with Billy because she could not understand what was going on and only knew what Billy had told her to understand.

The reason we chose to fight for a conservator was twofold.

First and foremost, Jean will most likely outlive Billy and she will need funds to continue living comfortably until her death. Knowing that she is disabled means she will probably need special care as she ages, and special care costs a lot of money. The only way to be able to care for her long into the future is to make sure that her money stays with her, not Billy.

Secondly, a hearing for request of a court-appointed conservator will expose what has happened to her finances since Billy took over. At this point in time we suspect that Billy is after her money, and all financial records will have to be submitted to the courts.

CHAPTER 15

Protecting Your Kingdom

Our primary goal in writing this book is to prevent others from experiencing the same losses we have by arming everyone with the knowledge and tools to have a fighting chance.

If it's not in writing, it didn't happen.

Looking back, I recall how our days were mentally excruciating. Every waking hour for Terrie and myself was filled with the terror and reality of what was happening to Jean and us. Eating was difficult at best, and each night I would lay with Terrie and hold her until her weeping turned to sleep.

Sleep was the only escape from the constant drumming of the events which had unfolded, except when the thoughts invaded my slumber and I would just bolt straight up in bed, the dream and the reality mixing into my conscious thought. It was inescapable, thoughts of dread for my wife, thoughts of horror for Jean, not knowing what she was doing, and thoughts of my-self trying with every part of my soul to keep it together, to be the strong one, knowing the road ahead was not going to make this living nightmare easier.

So many unanswered questions, not knowing what exactly was going to happen, and having absolutely no control of any-thing were the worst things we have ever had to deal with.

I had to stay strong. I had to trust that Matt would find a way to rescue us and Jean from what was appearing to be an ines-capable scenario. Trust was something I had run out of, with so many professionals who had proven incompetent to perform their duties, and knowing that there would be new profession-als entering the picture through the court proceedings, I was hyper-vigilant toward everyone connected to this case, even Matt. I even began to question my trust for my thoughts and feelings, normally a forward-thinking man, a leader of people through my profession, insightful to the positive strategies of life.

Now there were so many dark thoughts for those who had failed us; the kingdom I was responsible for had been invaded and I was helpless to protect it. I could not fight back and I was adrift as if I was in a dream, able to see everything crumbling around me—with my hands tied behind my back. The only thing that was clear to me was to be strong for Terrie, and it became my mantra, my thread of hope that pushed me forward.

Of course, Terrie was cleared of any wrongdoing by Elder Protection Services. They merely stated that she was cleared. Now if you tried to insert any common sense to the situation at this point, you would think that a government agency called Elder Protective Services would do something to immediately go after Billy now that they had all of the financial records and could see clearly that Billy had perpetrated this scheme. But no, their only job was to merely investigate and report.

Once the government becomes involved in the business of

your family, they apparently have the right to mess everything up, and they have no professional accountability in place to say to themselves, "Hey, we messed up big-time here and there is a disabled lady who has been abused." The agent at Elder Protection Services could see everything very clearly, and even more than they were letting on, because they are not required to say anything other than "she is cleared."

So what did they know? We would find out later that Billy had closed all of Jean's bank accounts and opened new ones, all the while telling Jean it was to make sure Terrie did not have access. According to him, Terrie was stealing from her. I could imagine all of the conniving conversations. He had conveniently put his name jointly on all of those accounts as well.

He had taken some bonds that had been given to Jean by her aunt and uncle and cashed them in. He put the considerable money into a new bank account at his personal bank with his and Jean's name on the account, but later took Jean's name off of that account. He had taken all of Jean's investments and invested them through another financial person with himself as the beneficiary. He had taken a life insurance policy out on Jean with, of course, himself as the beneficiary. There was another life insurance policy from Terrie's dad that was somehow overlooked by Jean at the time of his death that Terrie was the beneficiary of.

Billy had that transferred into his name as the beneficiary. He had even gone as far as to go to Jean's estate attorney and try to have the trust changed. Fortunately, Terrie had contacted this attorney right after the trap was sprung, and he had assured Terrie that he would not let anything happen to the trust at that time.

If you find yourself thrust into a tragic situation of any kind, it helps to have neutral and valuable team members on your side.

We visited with our counselor, Deanna, on a pretty regular basis throughout this dark time. She was so inspirational, thought-provoking, and always made us look into ourselves for answers while nurturing a peace within us. The universe works in such mysterious and wonderful ways. We both feel that, with Deanna, we were in the presence of someone who was sent to us for a reason early in our lives, but also knowing we would need the wisdom and encouragement to feel warm in our hearts for each other, yet strong and unwavering in our dedication toward the battle that had forced itself upon us. We are so very, very grateful for her.

The days passed slowly as we waited for the day Terrie could see the judge in an attempt to have the restraining orders taken away. We tried as best we could to make some normalcy for ourselves, diving into work, and in the day-to-day chores of urban life.

There were still sleepless and tearful nights as well as the tormenting days where nothing got done. We gave each other as much space as each of us needed to deal with our thoughts and our wavering motivations to take on what used to be so normal for us. The new normal was not happy, but rather, tolerant. This worked best and each of us did our part to comfort each other when the darkness was stronger than one of us could bear.

I can imagine that those who have had to face unthinkable adversity might turn on each other. It seems natural that there are some who for whatever reason cannot help but place some sort of blame on the other out of their own insecurity. There are always those who turn to friends or family for guidance and those people in turn are not equipped to handle the situation in guiding another human through such problems, and those in trouble grow away from each other.

Change happens so very quickly these days, and we believe that those who do not change together, change apart.

Terrie and I have always been encouraging to each other.

We recognized early on that change is necessary for growth

and that change is good for a healthy relationship. In addition to that formula, we have not only encouraged positive change in each other, but have also given each other the space necessary to make that change complete. Reversing roles for domestic chores, working harder to create additional income if the change meant a slowing of monetary gain, or recognizing that strict budgeting was key to withstand the time needed for a career change to come to fruition. Money is another one of those things that can tear at a relationship.

We learned many years ago how to be smart with our money. We do not use a credit card unless we can pay it off without interest. We pay cash for as many things as possible and always realize a discounted price for doing so. We purchased a home when the market was low and offered an exceptional price.

We refinanced our home when the financial timing was right, but did not take out extra funds, which defeats the purpose of spending money wisely; interest is the enemy, avoid it at all costs!

When we purchased our vacation home on the coast, we took equity from our main home to afford that down payment without having to spend cash reserves or take out a loan. Again, interest is the enemy. When the market crash came in the middle of the last decade, we pulled back by renting our vacation home rather than spending our cash reserves. We saw so many people go into debt trying to maintain their previous lifestyle while falling further and further into financial despair.

Home foreclosures were the telling signs of those who did not fully understand how precarious the market crash made everything. Just one setback financially and everything spiraled out of control for them. I feel so bad for those folks. Hard working and well intentioned people caught up in the circumstances of those unthinkable scoundrels who caused the crash in the first place, and apparently uninformed as to how best to avoid catastrophic loss. We all do the best we can, but sometimes we fall short and we have to build in to our lives the recognition and clarity that we will fall short at times. We are not rich by any means, just middle-class folks, but we have always lived happily within our means.

CHAPTER 16

Healing

If you've ever been affected by a traumatic situation, you know how difficult healing can be. But in the end it's our own healing that matters, and getting free from bondage and bitterness that can chain our souls is an important endeavor. Please seek professional guidance sooner than later.

What do you need to get free from? Write a letter, even if you never deliver it.

I was encouraged to write a letter to Billy, and here's what I came up with:

To: Billy
From: Jon
It was suggested that I write a letter expressing my thoughts of you and what you have done to my family be-

cause some think by doing this it will allow me some sense of relief by getting my feelings out.

You are a psychopath by every definition of the word. Your cowardly acts of greed perpetrated upon Jean are among the most despicable things one could do to another human being. It is obvious that you have no values or principles toward a life of fulfillment through hard work and good deeds, and have lived in such a reckless manner that has left you nothing in return.

So rather than reach down and pull yourself up, like men do, you prey on the loneliness of a woman. Then, you took your greed to another level and preyed on a lonely old woman who has had a traumatic brain injury just to get her money.

The flaw in your scheme is that you underestimated our resolve and resourcefulness to fight you. You tried to get the money, but you did not succeed. You live in squalor just like pigs do and that does not surprise me in the least. To make Jean live in that environment is just another testament to your psychopathic ways. You are the filth of the Earth and deserve to rot in your own undoing. You see, this is not how the universe works and you will pay for your criminal actions toward your fellow man for all of eternity. You will continue to suffer from your own devious actions until you die a wretched, lonely, death and what's left of your wretched soul will surely be spread to the furthest ends of the universe.

You are very fortunate in only one aspect of your treachery and that is that you did not do this 20 years ago when I was not as refined and enlightened as I am today. Things would have turned out very unfortunate for you then. Let me assure you however, that I will continue to fight your action until your death. I have made it one of my missions in life to warn others of predators such as you and to help *them see the lowly animal that stands before them and how to stop what atrocities may be thrust upon them. This is not a threat to you, but rather, a promise to myself.*

P.S. This letter has done nothing to diminish my resolve. The legal noose is continuing to tighten around your neck. Soon you will not be able to bear what you have brought upon yourself and the universe shall be merciless in exacting your punishment.

Have a great day!

Jon

Whether you agree with it or not, it's my letter, and my healing. No doubt I've been angry, and sad, and frustrated, and upset. When will it stop? Healing is a continuum, and no matter what tragedy or challenges you face in your own life, you have to process it on your own. You'll feel a variety of emotions, but the trick is to not get overwhelmed. Lean on your loved ones.

Don't get overwhelmed by the what-ifs, or the negative. Focus on the living and the people you can help. We wanted to write this book together to let you know that you have a choice. You can let tragedy divide your family, or cement it together. We've faced this challenge with differing emotions at times, because it's Terrie's mother, not mine. But the challenge has brought us closer together.

Terrie wrote her own letter, only hers would be directed to her mother. Here it is, from her perspective. She misses her mother. It's just as simple as that. And she grieves for what could have been.

When she was asked to write her mom a letter, it was a painful, gutwrenching process.

Dear Mom,

I wish you were still part of our family. I miss you.

I think back of how things used to be, before the acci-

dent, all the happy memories we shared. It was great you and Dad both being teachers, we spent all those summers as kids camping and traveling back to North Dakota to visit grandparents. We saw a lot of places over the years, and I feel fortunate to have those memories.

I remember a long time ago when Jon and I were first married. I took a week's vacation and you and I spent that whole time re-upholstering that old couch. We swore we'd never do anything like that again but we got it done. I remember every Christmas we'd make tons of cookies at your house.

Dad would be there hanging around waiting for them to come out of the oven—happy times and happy memories. I remember those Thanksgiving holidays we all spent together at that cabin at the coast. We'd go out Thanksgiving morning looking for plant materials to make the centerpiece for the dinner table. You always decorated so beautifully for all of the holidays. I remember after Dad died when you and I went to the ranch and painted the whole house, just the two of us. That was a lot of work and it took days, but we did it. We made a pretty good team.

I remember how you used to have a song for everything and I could always tell whether you were happy or not when you would be singing. It's so sad that you're not a part of our lives anymore and I want you to know what really happened. You were taken advantage of when you were at your weakest. It's hard to comprehend what brain injuries, especially one as severe as yours, can do to people.

I would never have believed that you would turn away from your family to be with Billy. I wish you would have talked to us, given us a chance. You need to know that Billy helped you to believe that I was stealing from you. Billy was the one that lied to the judge to get the restraining orders against me.

He was the one who called Elder Protective Services and told them I was stealing money from you. Billy was the one who had his financial advisor change all of your investment accounts and name himself as the beneficiary. Billy was the one who had you cash those savings bonds you treasured; he put them in a joint account at his bank and Mom, days after the conservatorship hearing where you were deemed subject to undue influence, he took your name off that account.

I want you to know that everything bad that happened here was because of Billy. You were a great Mother, you were supportive and loving and my best friend. I wish I could tell you that but all the authorities all along the way, the police officer, the judge, your attorney and most importantly Billy all made sure that I could have no contact with you when it was so important that I did.

The longer that I was unable to talk to you the more they were able to drive the wedge between us. It was Billy who hired his own attorney for you and what he's done to keep us apart and destroy our relationship is unthinkable. I know that you'll probably never read this, but I hope that you're happy; I hope he's treating you well. You deserve nothing but the best, you always have.

The end. That's it. Is that it?

TERRIE'S VIEW

When I wrote that letter it shattered me for days. That's how I knew I needed to do it.

The process of letting go may be something you need to accept. I am really sad about losing my mother in such a way. It's something you never expect, because I didn't lose her to death, or even to the car accident. I just lost her unexpectedly.

After all these years to have her influenced like she was after her head injury in that car wreck, it really is sad.

I miss the old family traditions.

Christmas Eve we ate the same food every year, homemade clam chowder and pita sandwiches with deli meat. We celebrated Christmas Eve with the family. Before the presents were opened, one of us would read from a book that was brought out every year; it had all kinds of Christmas traditions, crafts, and the story of the very first Christmas.

Then it was time for the presents; even the dogs got a gift. But it wasn't over on Christmas Eve.

Christmas morning we got up and were back at their house by 10 a.m. Wonderful smells were coming from the kitchen and breakfast was just about ready. Again, the food would be much the same each year, crepes with cherries, bacon, scrambled eggs, and pull-apart cinnamon bread. But before breakfast we all headed downstairs and opened stockings. Santa kept coming even though we were grown. Santa visited all the relatives at this house, young or old.

One would think that would be enough celebrating of Christmas, but no, there was still Christmas dinner. We'd leave after the breakfast dishes had been cleaned and then head to our house to prepare Christmas dinner for everyone. The meal wasn't the same; it varied from year to year. We'd go all out with decorating and making the table look as beautiful as possible.

Mom's table was always beautifully set with her mother's crystal dishes. She treasured them, and Dad and my son Dereck had built a glass cabinet so that she could display them there. After Christmas came birthdays; my dad's and mine were on the same day in January, so Mom would bake two cakes, one white and one chocolate, the same every year until he died.

In fact every holiday was really a celebration with family— Valentine's Day, Easter, Fourth of July, we came together. After Dad died, Mom was really lost for several years. She spent a lot of time with us; now Sunday dinners took place in our home.

I knew that she wasn't cooking much anymore so I'd send her home with leftovers every week. We never moved far from my parents; we wanted to be able to help them as they grew older, that was the plan. After Dad was gone it was really nice that we were just minutes from her house. I could have walked there if I had to.

Our lives were so certain. If she needed help with something around the house, Jon stepped in. I thought that's just how life would be! Mom and us moving through the years, helping her more as she needed it and being there with her, until the end. I never thought that there'd be a car accident that would change her and us forever.

After Dad died, she eventually developed a new routine. She went to church every Sunday and volunteered there too. She was in charge of prepping for communions and had a group of women she coordinated with to make sure everything—hundreds of little wine glasses, trays and linens—were washed and properly put away.

She went to Starbucks every afternoon at 4, Monday through Friday. Even if she and I had just had coffee an hour before when we parted she was off to Starbucks to visit with her regular group of friends she'd come to know. Three days a week she went to the gym and worked out with her trainer Janet. She even went on some Elder-hostel trips by herself, once to Scotland for several weeks.

Several years after Dad died she started to take dance classes, and that's where she met Billy. Of course, I've already said this before. I've said it a multitude of times and it keeps replaying in my mind, over and over like a broken record.

I keep remembering the tiny details, Christmases, Birthdays, the way she wore her hair.

And that's how it is with tragedy. You go over it again and again.

CHAPTER 17

Hindsight

Where are you in your healing? Or maybe this book is for someone you know, and it can change their life or make them more aware of the things that can happen when a loved one gets diagnosed with dementia or a brain injury.

Looking back, I see that there were warning signs along the way, yet I was too focused on my mother's emotional well-being to pay attention. One was my mother's hesitancy to introduce her new man to us, even though we had a very close relationship. Why wouldn't she? Unless she'd been coached not to.

My mother didn't let on for a long time, that she was actually dating anyone. We were pretty surprised when she said that she'd met a man at the dance classes and that they were dating. But she seemed happier and that was important, because she hadn't been happy for a long time and we wanted that for her.

So, I overlooked the fact that she'd hid it.

After about a year or so into their relationship, she and Billy did come over to our house. It was summertime, I remember, because we sat out on the back porch.

It was awkward, trying to strike up a conversation with him. He seemed like a nice enough guy, but they didn't stay long enough to get much of a sense of him. I doubt they were even there an hour. Jon was concerned about Billy right away. He sensed something that I didn't. That was another warning sign, because my husband has great gut instincts.

As much as I asked Mom to have Billy join us for holidays, she never did. That should have been another warning sign that prompted us to take greater control of things before they changed.

As time went by, Mom became more and more attached to Billy. She would drive down to his house every night, rain or shine. It was a 45-minute trip and I often thought, *How could he let her do that, wouldn't it be better for him to drive to her home if he wanted to see her?* A red flag for sure.

She always explained that he had to work and it was more convenient for him if she were to go there. I think he had it pretty good because she'd come whenever he called.

I know that the world is made up of all kinds of families. Some homes are filled with laughter. Some of them fight with each other, and some families have rifts and never speak to each other. It seems such a waste; life is so short and people spend it apart. But I never thought my life with my mother would end like this. I could never have dreamed that someone she knew, a stranger to me, would be a person who could be so cruel and separate a person from her family and make her believe the worst of us. Looking back, I can see how Jon was right about Billy. Jon had great insight and discernment early on.

Billy is a man who had ulterior motives, saw an opportunity, and jumped at it.

We would later learn at the hearing that Billy testified in court that he was the one who called Elder Protective Services and that he was the one who called the police. He was the one who had Mom close her bank accounts.

At the time, after the accident, I was holding savings bonds at our house for her while she was living there, and kept them for safety while there were caretakers in the house. I had to turn them over along with my ledger and other original paperwork I was keeping for her.

Those bonds were quickly cashed in the amount of approximately $50,000, and according to their attorney, Mr. Cook, they opened a joint bank account at U.S. Bank. After we successfully won the conservatorship hearing, he took my mother's name off that account. He created this ruse of theft against me just to get me out of the way so that he could do all of those things.

He's the one who masterminded this whole thing. He's the one who kept her away from church, he kept her from friends, and he cancelled her gym membership and her credit card. He just took it upon himself to do all of these things. He had her put the house up for sale. He's the one that was moving everything into his name by influencing her to do it all. Some people said that Billy was such a nice guy; we think he's a villain. Matt thinks he's a psychopath. Billy is the puppet master here.

My feelings have been a roller coaster, from sad, to angry, to sad again at what I've lost. I'm really not sad about this anymore, but I am really angry. Yet in time, I know it'll heal as I see the ways in which we help other families avoid the same kind of emotional roller coaster.

I keep going back in my head to that terrible day, July 1, when I called my mom's cell phone and Officer Powers answered. I couldn't believe it. That day an officer said that Mom had accused me of stealing large amounts of money from her. It felt like she had already decided that I'd done something wrong. I don't know what standard operating procedure is for law enforcement, but if that's the protocol it needs to be improved. Here Officer Powers was sitting with the man who would ultimately play a critical role in destroying my family, and she told me that they just looked like a cute, doting couple.

She told me that my Mom didn't want to see me and that I shouldn't go over there. How could that be? How could she so distrust me? Looking back at it now and knowing how brain injuries can affect different people, I can easily see how it happened.

She had developed a long-term relationship with a virtual stranger to us, succumbed to his charms because of her loneliness, and with her brain now damaged, he had over the past two months, convinced her that we were all out to get her.

She believed every last detail he told her, and she would think of other possible scenarios and he would reinforce them as realities. During the recovery time she spent at our house, I saw flickers of that but didn't realize what lay ahead. On Mother's Day we sat down to open presents. We gave ours to her and she went through the motions of opening it up and then just dropped it to the floor, picked up her phone, and went to her room. We could hear that she had called Billy. It was so bizarre.

We both looked at each other and said, "What was that all about?" Looking at the clock we could see it was 7, so it didn't take much to deduce he'd told her to call him at 7.

Once she was done talking with him she came back out, picked up the gift as if nothing had ever happened, and gushed about how nice it was. We were more than surprised at this behavior. As she continued to stay with us I could see just how, not frantic, but overly expectant she was about the possibility of receiving or getting to make a call to him. When she was on the phone she sounded as if it was a totally different person who'd just left my living room.

She suddenly became overly happy and cheery, even if she were bemoaning the fact to me that she didn't feel like herself just minutes ago.

I couldn't figure it out; why such a great fake? Such a great effort to pretend she was normal? Not to lose him, of course.

I just didn't know to what end she would go, to give up her family to ensure that happened. He must have known it too; it was more than obvious.

There's another person that makes me sad and also mad and that's the woman with the in-home care company. When Dr. Nguyen, the neurosurgeon, decided after seeing Mom toward the end of May that she was able to be at home with a caregiver, we interviewed several companies. Mom was there with us at her house. The first two companies were rather unimpressive.

When Marge came in I got a good vibe from her; she was well spoken, paid good attention to Mom, and seemed like a very bright, caring individual.

We hired her company and made the arrangements to have caregivers come to stay with Mom. There would be three different people assigned a twelve-hour shift throughout the week. Marge was there the first morning when we met the first new caregiver.

I thought I had added another capable member of our team to help Mom, but that wasn't the case at all. In the beginning she acted as if I was in charge and communicated with me regularly. I never suspected that while she was acting one way with me, she was also developing a relationship with Billy.

On July 5, when Marge called me, she said that she couldn't talk with me anymore about the senior care or anything for that matter. She said that Mom and Billy were revoking my power of attorney and that Billy had power of attorney for Mom now. I told her that I was going to have to pursue a conservatorship for Mom and she said that she totally understood. Little did I know that she would go straight to Billy and tell him that same thing.

As the months passed, Marge somehow became the go-between for us, Mom, and Billy. Whenever they wanted something communicated, she would call. One day in October she called to say that Mom was going to sell her house and that they were going to have an estate sale because she didn't want anything. What?!

That wasn't my mother! My mother treasured her family heirlooms, her photo albums, her mother's dishes; her guest room was a tribute to her childhood, with many of her toys on display for guests to see. There was a trunk from a great-grand-parent, her own parents' things, and the piano she used to play. In every room of that house there was something from family that had been passed down and she treasured it all. Now suddenly she didn't want any of it?!

I questioned Marge about Mom suddenly not wanting any of her family items and she said that they weren't important to her anymore. Unbelievable! I asked her to have Mom call me and Marge said my mother didn't want to talk to me. It was during that phone conversation that Marge also shared that she no longer worked for the senior care company. When I asked why she was still involved with Mom, she told me it was because she promised her she'd help.

She went on to say that I could come over and put sticky notes on the things that I'd like. Even though it seemed absolutely crazy to me, we made the arrangements to do it several weeks later. On that day she followed me around while I put a sticky note here and there on furniture and pieces that I knew my parents wanted to stay in the family.

I find it interesting and very telling that just a few months after Billy married my mother, Marge quit her job at senior care company.

I believe it's because she knew what she'd done was wrong.

She'd authorized one of her staff to actually fly with them to Las Vegas so that they could get married. My mother needed that much help. I wonder what she got out of this because surely one wouldn't put their job on the line for an act as terrible as that. She actually authorized one of her staff to coordinate flights and hotel reservations for a person in their care, who they knew was incapacitated, so that she could fly to another state and marry without the family knowing.

In November Marge called to say that the items from Mom's house that they were letting me have were in the garage. Marge said that Mom didn't want people tramping all over her house. We had to meet Marge on a Sunday morning at Mom's garage so that she could let us in. It was demeaning. When she finally let us into the garage, there wasn't much there. Some china and childhood toys, but mostly stuff that you'd see in a garage sale; we left most of it there.

In the spring, and during the conservatorship hearing while Mom was testifying, it came up that she didn't want "receivership" as she called it, rather than a conservatorship. At that hearing, before it started, there was Marge sitting all cozy with Billy. It took me back to the conversation in July when I told her I was thinking about conservatorship. She had gone to Billy and he'd used it to further separate Mom from us.

Claudia was in on it too; she was one of the original caregivers who had shifts with Mom several times a week. In July when Mom and Billy petitioned the judge for restraining orders against me, it was Claudia who actually stood up and testified in a court of law that I was stealing large amounts of money from my mother.

Why would someone do that? I'd had several phone conversations with her. Claudia told me that Mom didn't think she needed caregivers but that she needed more time to rest and heal. Claudia told me that Mom didn't think she needs caregivers but that she didn't realize how forgetful she was, or how much she no longer understood how to do simple tasks. Then, in court, she lied about me. She too quit before summer's end because I'm sure, again, she knew the wrong she had done.

The decision of the judge on that day in July allowed the permanent separation of my mother from her family to be cast in stone. When I called the judge's office to try to complain, I was told by her assistant that the judge bases her facts on what she hears in court that day. What she heard were lies.

There's food for thought and something quite scary if you think about it long enough. How many other judges around the country base their decisions of that day on what they've heard from whoever was standing before them? During the conservatorship hearing, Billy admitted that he'd stood up in court on that July day and falsely accused me.

Judges may be hearing lies that affect the lives of others forever. There is something very concerning about our justice system. It was the first of many instances that would continue to reverberate as we moved through this ordeal.

What can people learn from this?

Number one on our list is to put your affairs in order starting today, and question the experts. I've been through numerous personality tests through different companies I've worked for during different points in time. I've had a handful of those tests over the years that remained pretty consistent with respect to the results even though the jobs have changed. Test results have shared I was concrete, sequential, amiable, analytical, enjoyable, logical, and most recently, a banker.

Meaning I follow the rules, I do what's right, I do my job with the best of my abilities, I believe the experts to be experts in the field of their choice, and in my mind, I am supposed to trust them. But what I have found over these past few years is that this is not always the case.

When faced with a TBI, or any emergency for that matter, one needs to seek out all the help and advice that they possibly can. We had no idea what to expect; the doctors only told us that she might get better. When we took Mom home from the hospital, other than some basic instructions, all they gave us was a handout that had a list of potential caregivers. They didn't tell us that her mental state may have changed, they didn't mention anything about the fact that her confusion may lead to distrust.

No one said that she might display obsessive behavior. They didn't bring up that she might easily become susceptible to the influences of others. What they did say was that her short term memory might never recover; that the first few months were critical to that. They did say that they weren't sure when, or if, she would ever be back to her normal mental capacity. They did tell us that it could take up to a year before one could ascertain if an individual would fully recover, or if their mental capacity at that time is as far as they would ever progress. I wish I had known more and understood better about brain injuries. During her sessions with the occupational therapist, I started to get some sense of the depth of her injury. The therapist always went through a series of tests.

Looking back, it's easier to see more clearly, although there were so many things out of our control.

When Mom had therapy there were memory exercises, some logical . . . one in particular was to draw the face of a clock and put the hands in place that would show the time of day. After the accident and those sessions, Mom would spend long periods of time drawing clocks until she'd get so frustrated that she'd give up. I never saw her draw a clock correctly again.

That seems to be a basic test the therapists give. I can remember her saying to me one afternoon, "I can't believe I have to learn how to draw a clock all over again." People need to know that a TBI can change a person's personality, and can change what they feel is important in life.

CHAPTER 18

Realities

People need to know that no matter how much we would like or hope it to be, nothing in life is certain. Especially when other people are involved in a position of authority over us.

We were having dinner with friends one evening recently, discussing the subject of accidents. It's something we do because we are passionate about helping people to prepare for that life event that they hope will never happen. A girlfriend shared that she had told her teenage daughters not to worry, she wasn't going anywhere. People seem to have such a certainty that nothing will happen to them. But our story is proof that anything can happen to anyone.

Maybe it's because a lot has happened to us that we want to get the word out. Why not prepare for that just in case? It's those hundreds of little things that you don't even think about.

As an example, do you have a post office box? Does a family member know that? Do you receive checks there? How would they know that if something happened to you? It's really alarming to think that so many people are unprepared for life's uncertainties and eventualities. Whether a person chooses to believe it or not, the reality is that there are thousands of people every day who lose a loved one to an accident or sudden illness.

The father of a family friend passed quite suddenly. He was vibrant and full of life in his early 70s. But after a brief illness, he was gone. At the funeral we spoke to his wife, who shared that she was so grateful for helping them to get his affairs organized. They are such a loving family! You see this very intelligent man used acronyms to code all of his passwords. Because they had time to decipher them, they were able to access all of the finances and other items he used to take care of. Without that valuable information it could have taken months for her to figure out, if she was ever able to at all.

We wrote this book because people need to know that they have to put their affairs in order not just to protect themselves, but the family they love, and they need to do it while they are clear-minded.

If you haven't created a legal plan of action for yourself and your family, it needs to be made a priority. One might think that the cost is too much. The cost is much greater if it's left undone, and possibly catastrophic in many families. The point is, all of these things must be carefully thought through and put in writing with the proper signatures and in proper form, which an estate attorney can do for you once you pull all of the information together. Just start by typing out everything you own onto a password-protected flash drive. Passwords, furnishings, real estate, pet info, Veteran contact info, insurances, where to find the gold buried in the backyard! Everything. Contact information should accompany all organizations you work with. Not having these will be a great source of cost and frustration for someone you love.

You can control a flash drive; you cannot control the Internet. We do not believe information of this type should ever be kept on the cloud somewhere. We have owned a secured website business and know with good expertise that the Internet is under attack for sites which store confidential customer information.

I wish I could take you step by step here, but every family has a different dynamic as well as a different plan of action.

Since Mom's accident and everything that's happened afterward, we've shared our story with just a few other people. It has caused us to look back and replay the events of the past few years, over and over again, when we'd rather not relive it. But if reliving it helps someone else, it turns our loss into a gain.

JON

When it came to Jean's property, we had been caught unaware. It is Real Estate 101 for any Realtor to find out the disposition of ownership of a property in order to clear it for sale. Matt contacted the new attorney for Jean and inquired as to the sale. Mr. Cook agreed that this had not been done. Funny how the attorney for Jean, who had obviously seen the Trust, did not have the Realtor call Terrie, but rather just went forward with the sale . . . very complicit of him, in our opinion. Terrie called the Realtor and confronted her on the sale and why she had not caught the Trust issue. The Realtor said she was sorry, but the property had an accepted offer. Terrie explained that she may have an offer, but the Trust would control the proceeds. Interestingly, the Realtor said that Jean and Billy were hoping to build a log cabin on Billy's property with the proceeds.

Well, isn't that convenient for Billy?! Sell Jean's home, build a new home on his land, and most likely not put Jean on the deed. Through the hearings we found that he had put his name on her investment and bank accounts, and in one instance had even taken her name off of a bank account!

Again, prudence on Terrie's part had thwarted this latest attempt to take money from Jean. Another professional, the Realtor, not doing a basic component of her job.

There were many discussions regarding the property between the attorneys, and Jean's attorney seemed to think that the sale was just fine. In the end, Terrie agreed to move forward with the sale, but the proceeds would be held until the determination of the conservator was made.

Finally, the day of the conservatorship hearing had arrived.

Terrie and I went out for breakfast near the courthouse. It was a rainy morning, which seemed to fit the day's proceedings and everything that had happened since the car wreck. The courthouse was in the county that Billy and Jean now live in, about 15 miles from our home. It's a small, old courthouse with an old metal detector at the door. It was cold and dark inside, reflecting the weather conditions outside, as we made our way up to the floor where the proceedings would take place.

We met Matt there and briefly went over his presentation one more time. He would present his case first, then Jean's attorney would present her case, and both attorneys would present closing arguments.

Matt told us he had done some checking and found that the attorney representing Jean was Billy's longtime attorney, Mr. Cook. He said that Billy had retained him for other matters in the past. Well, isn't that just great? Now this attorney was representing Jean in the matter of a conservatorship to protect Jean's financial well-being from Billy, and Jean is represented by Billy's attorney. Common sense would dictate that this is wrong, but the court system is a fickle entity.

As part of the pretrial information gathering, Matt had Jean see an expert psychologist to perform a mental evaluation of Jean to determine exactly what her clinical mental state of mind was at the current time. Doctor Hearst was highly regarded in this field of work and had run a battery of tests with Jean. This must have been terrifying for her.

As we approached the courtroom, there was Jean sitting with about ten other people whom we didn't know.

Jean looked up and smiled, saying, "That's my daughter." It was eerie to see her smiling like she was glad to see Terrie, like nothing had happened. She was genuinely happy to see Terrie.

I looked at each of the other people sitting with Jean. I wanted to make direct eye contact with each of them to see if they knew that I knew what was really happening here. Each of them looked down at their feet or away when I looked at them. They were all criminals and they all knew it. I didn't see Billy anywhere, but knew he would surely be there.

Our son had arrived just as we were ready to enter the courtroom. I was so very happy that he had come to support Terrie and myself. This had also been quite devastating to him as well. Consider that this had all happened to him, too. He lost his only uncle as a boy, then his grandfather dies, and now he was about to sit in on a hearing for all of the things which had been perpetrated against his grandmother and listen to false accusations about his mother.

Certainly, this is not what he would have expected after being so close to Jean, as her only grandson. A life of family being close to each other in all things, moving through the ups and downs of life, and then losing people close to him. He has been very strong through this nightmare.

He takes after Terrie, inasmuch as not demonstrating his emotions outwardly, unlike his father. He appears to let stuff just roll off of his back and takes things in stride. I'm glad he has these traits and they have served him well in his life. He has been a spectator in all of this, a cruel fact that can only be terrifying . . . to watch his parents have to go through everything that has happened. We have tried the best we can to tell him everything that has happened in real time. Having only one child, we have always lived with this type of open communication and included him in everything regarding our lives. I wish he did not have to go through this.

Protecting our children is important, but at the same time, not hiding the realities of life will hopefully prepare them for how to be strong in the face of adversity. The good and the bad, the grandiose and the macabre, for better or for worse, I am hopeful that he sees that the true love of two people is a balancing act that will survive if you just stick together in unity, no matter what.

We entered the courtroom at the far end from the judge's bench. Our son and I sat directly behind where Matt and Terrie were sitting. Jean and her attorney, Mr. Cook, sat next to Matt and Terrie. Jean looked bewildered, not even looking at Terrie. Mr. Cook was wearing a brown suit with the tail of his coat frayed as if it were the only one he had. His briefcase was very old and torn around the edges.

Even now, thinking about the lack of control and the idiocy, it is just all so hard to accept.

Another woman came in and sat near us; I assume it is Jess, the conservator we have been told so much about by Matt. She was dressed rather eclectically in layers of brightly colored fabrics. Her dress reminded me of someone from the sixties, Haight Ashbury style.

I looked over the crowd, and there to my astonishment was Marge, the caretaker manager. She was all cuddled up with Billy and looked like a shell of the person we hired to care for Jean. Her hair was dirty and messed, her clothes wrinkled, and her face looked to have aged several years. She cozied up to Billy like a little girl who had just awoken and was still a little sleepy. She looked up and saw I was looking at her. She looked down again as if she did not want to be there, but was compelled to do so. Such a strange, disconcerting memory.

In all of the madness of those initial days of Billy's grand scheme, Marge had obviously been swayed by Billy to be a part of his cadre of stooges. We are not sure what she got out of all of this.

We have not seen the storage unit where presumably all of Jean's furnishings are being kept, but hopefully after this hearing, we will gain access to that through the conservator.

So what was Marge doing here? Looking like a poor waif instead of a vibrant woman climbing the corporate ladder of a healthcare company. Had Billy pulled his stuff on her, too, after she had abetted him? Was he holding her hostage for the acts she had perpetrated on Jean and us? Had Billy threatened to turn her in for her part? Was there something even more sordid going on? We just couldn't figure it all out.

Terrie had called the care company at one point and found out that Marge was no longer employed there. Had she received enough compensation to leave, or was she still in some kind of deal with Billy? Nonetheless, she looked like hell and she was sitting too close to Billy, and that was all I needed to know at the time.

The proposed conservator, Jess, was referred to us by Matt. He has been around a long time and thought that Jess would be a good fit based on her reputation as a good conservator and her holding a PhD in gerontology. If there was any chance of Jean having a relationship with Terrie down the road, Jess would be able to massage that together. Terrie seemed to embrace this possibility, but I was skeptical of this ever happening. Of course, I am skeptical of everything regarding this situation after so much muddy water has passed under the bridge.

Jean's financial advisor, Sherrie, came in and sat next to our son and myself. Sherrie has always been of great importance to Jean. She is one of those people you want on your professional team, very astute toward her profession and so personable to her clients. Jean has used her for years and Sherrie has gone out of her way to help Jean any way she can, especially since the wreck.

Billy and the others who would testify were not allowed to be in the courtroom until after they had testified. I did see Jean's estate attorney, Bill Best, and Jack Grimes, the injury attorney I had hired to represent Jean regarding the wreck. I could only assume that they would be testifying for Jean. We all stood as the judge entered the courtroom and now the moment had arrived, the facts and the truth to be discovered and revealed. Both attorneys give their opening statements and then Matt called his first witness—Jess, the conservator.

If you have never been involved in a court hearing, there are some things you need to know. First off, common sense does not apply. It is each side doing whatever they can to win and it can get ugly. For instance, Terrie has only been interested in fighting for a conservator for two reasons: 1) so Billy doesn't take all of Jean's money, and 2) so that her mother has the money she needs to live out her life without financial burden. However, in court, Mr. Cook's line of questioning was strictly to show that Terrie is only trying to protect her inheritance. Even though Terrie has never done anything that would indicate anything other than love for her mother, Mr. Cook would be ruthless and even less than truthful, in order to attempt to show that Terrie's only motives were selfish ones.

Attorneys will do everything they can to try and discredit a witness's testimony as well. One witness might say they did something on a certain date, and the attorney would say, "What day of the week was that?" If the witness does not know, the attorney will have their "aha" moment by saying, "How can you be sure of the date when you don't even know what day it is?" Casting doubt is the name of the game.

As is always the case, if you have anything in your legal past you may not be proud of, an attorney will find those things out and it will be used against you in ways you can't imagine.

For instance, let's say hypothetically that you had a DUI as a teenager 20 years ago. Sure, you went through all of the stuff that one is supposed to do to learn not to do that again, and you have never driven after drinking again. But in court that can be used to shine light on how "irresponsible" you are, what "poor judgment" you have, how you have "no regard for your life or the lives of others," how you must have "poor self-esteem," and how you "cannot be trusted" with anything ever again. In fact, they might say with all that you did in your past, you are probably lying on the stand right now. Get the picture? Fortunately, Terrie and I have lived pretty squeaky clean lives, so there was nothing that could be twisted like that. Just one more reason to keep one's nose clean, as they say.

I know one important lesson that I would suggest to everyone to heed is don't touch the money! Even if you have power of attorney for your parent(s), don't touch the money until you have talked with, and had documented through an attorney, that you need to take that action and want to perform the task to the letter of the law. If there is anyone else who has intentions on getting that money, or even feels that they are somehow entitled to that money, they will make themselves visible at some point. You had better have taken the correct steps from day one, or you will be tested to the nth degree, and most likely in court. We have learned so much about greed through this experience, and how anyone can make any claim against you if they think the money should be theirs. We have heard many horror stories of siblings coming out of nowhere to abuse a parent, or contest a will, and it can get ugly and expensive.

Even a maid or next door neighbor can get in the mix, stating that they were promised some additional compensation by the elder person before they died. They may produce some letter stating so. Don't touch the money until you have the documentation and an attorney on your side.

This would also apply to how long you need to exercise the

power of attorney status. If you feel that you will need to facilitate the financial needs of a loved one, please consider hiring a third party accountant to review your ledgers monthly. You may even want to petition for a conservatorship as we did, just so that nobody can ever accuse you of not doing it correctly or accuse you of theft. There are several types of accounting and anyone can challenge you at any time. You may be doing things just right, but if someone challenges you on it and has "lawyered up," it could cost you a ton of money in attorney fees and court costs just to prove yourself.

Jess was great on the stand, a very confident woman with state and national affiliations regarding her profession. She keeps a small caseload in order to be available for her clients and takes a holistic approach to performing her job. When Mr. Cook got to her on redirect, he was more concerned with her being able to handle things until Jean got better and could do her own finances again.

Matt called Dr. Hearst to the stand next. Dr. Hearst explained in great detail how the assessment process is given. It is a complex series of tests to ascertain every aspect of one's cognitive abilities, including motor skills testing to see how the brain translates information to everyday tasks such as walking and writing. The writing tests are similar to those Jean was taking at the hospital right after the wreck, such as drawing a picture of a clock, for instance. There are accepted standards of testing in this field of work through the court system and Dr. Hearst appeared to have covered all the bases, from this layman's view. The doctor is very methodical in his mannerisms and delivery of his findings. He is older, with a thin build. He seems very efficient in his speech and reminds me of an old television detective I watched as a boy: "Just the facts, Ma'am, Just the facts."

After explaining the process, Dr. Hearst gave the court his findings. There are many terms and numbers thrown around that judges and attorneys understand, but much of it is psychobabble to me. The two statistics that stood out the most were Jean's cognitive functions, which Dr. Hearst described as in the lower one percentile for someone of her age. The other statistics he provided was her Intelligence Quotient (IQ), and he explained that Jean tested at an IQ level of a seven-year-old.

CHAPTER 19

Cognitive Function

It had been nearly one year since the wreck, and Jean did not seem to have improved much since then. It really took ahold of me as well why she had acted the way she did after the wreck, just like a child at times, only with the memories of a seventy-five-year-old. Now, I am not a doctor or psychologist, but from what we have experienced, cognitive function altered by a traumatic brain injury is much more than just the memories of what was just said or done. It can affect the memory of everyday functions that were once ingrained knowledge. I would imagine that if I looked down right now and realized I could not tie my shoes, even though I have been doing it all of my life, and you tried to teach me how but I would forget each time, it would be quite disconcerting, indeed.

My own mother is currently residing in the memory care

ward of a very nice center designed to care for people with dementia disorders. Mom has Alzheimer's disease. The disease is slow, and cruel, and will eventually end her life. I love her so much. It pains me to watch her slow deterioration.

With Jean's injury, it was fast, and random as to how it manifested itself. Of course, we were only with her for that first three months. While our concern that she might die from her injuries was high on the priority list for most of that time, I truly wish someone at the hospital or some resource or another had been able to tell us all of the ways the injury might affect her. But all we got was, "You'll have to wait and see because she might get better."

Mr. Cook had a chance to re-examine Dr. Hearst's testimony and went through the usual items you would expect a defense attorney to address. Have you ever tested a woman of her age? Are you sure you tested properly? Are you sure you are not drawing false conclusions? But then Mr. Cook started down a line of questioning that flew in the face of what Dr. Hearst had testified to.

Questions like: "Isn't it true that you are only coming to your conclusions because you were hired by the opposing attorney? Is it true that you make most of your living by appearing in court cases? Isn't it true that Ms. Barnes (Jean's maiden name), is able to live a full and productive life even though she has some minor memory problems just like most elderly people do?" This was Mr. Cook's role, to ask questions that would shine a bit of doubt on the doctor. Mr. Cook was so animated in his delivery it was almost comical, yet Dr. Hearst stood firm on his abilities and the findings he had testified too.

Terrie was up next. She explained her lifelong history with Jean and how she had helped Jean before and after the wreck. When Mr. Cook had the chance to cross examine, he just made up stuff like: "You really had a rocky relationship with your mother, didn't you?" "You have hated Billy all along and that's why you never kept him in the loop about what was happening to your mother after she was injured, isn't that true?"

Then, he tried to use the fact that Jean had been gifting us annually for many years to shelter her tax burden, as if Terrie had been forcing her to do that. The fact is Jean had brought that to our attention years ago after meeting with her financial advisor and estate lawyer, Bill Best. Jean had been gifted by her father for decades as well; it's what their family did in an effort to be smart with their money. Mr. Cook kept badgering Terrie until the judge finally asked him to stop.

Sherrie was on the stand next. She went through her professional relationship with Jean and how she had managed her finances for many years. She also backed up the gifting question as a regular financial decision made by families across the country to avoid paying that money to the government. Mr. Cook badgered Sherrie for quite a while too. It did not seem he was creating doubt about Sherrie, but rather was trying to implicate her in trying to sway Jean into making financial decisions that did not make sense. Matt did a good job on re-cross examination to have Sherrie explain all of the meetings she had with Jean after the wreck and how she had even personally checked up on Jean weekly to see how she was doing. It was appalling to us how Mr. Cook could try to twist a life of financial tradition within a family into something it was not. Seeing as Jean could not think up such a scheme, it was apparent Mr. Cook was devising it on his own.

When it was Mr. Cook's turn to call witnesses, he called up Jean's estate attorney, Bill Best. Bill explained his relationship with Jean and how he had come to know Billy. Remember, Bill was one of the people Terrie called right after the accident and right after Billy had made his move. When our attorney Matt had him on cross examination, Mr. Best told of Billy coming to his office trying to change Jean's family trust. This was the one time I saw Jean actually react to anything that had been said in the courtroom up to this point. Matt also had Mr. Best talk about his knowledge of Terrie, to which he was most kind.

Next on the stand was another attorney, Mr. Dill, who was there only to try and shed doubt upon Dr. Hearst's testimony. He told of certain tests that swayed results to show evidence that would only benefit a client, and how Dr. Hearst made a lot of money from being a case witness. When Matt had him in cross examination, it turned out that this lawyer had to admit that Dr. Hearst had not used those types of tests on Jean.

Next up for Mr. Cook was the accident attorney, Mr. Jack Grimes. He explained how I had contacted him and facilitated the contract to represent Jean. Then Mr. Cook went down a line of questioning that the accident attorney could only answer about Terrie's and my disdain for Billy. He did this in a way that presented Billy as the poor boyfriend shunned by the family, defending Billy while supposedly representing Jean. On cross examination, Matt had him explain his meetings with Jean and the contract signed for his payment. It was difficult to hear him say on one hand how cognizant Jean was that day, knowing he would have to represent her in the accident case where he would have to show how terribly diminished her cognitive impairments were.

Let me present a side note, something about the court system.

Matt had talked several times about how "presentable" Jean was, another term for cute, little old lady. Apparently her being presentable meant that there was a physical perception that the cute, little old lady was so nice, how could anything be wrong? "Presentable," meaning that these professionals would assume that the cute, little old lady just had to be in control. But more interestingly, it was a situation where attorneys don't want to be perceived as beating up the cute, little old lady on the witness stand.

Mr. Cook then called Jean to the stand. Jean sat down after

identifying herself and then proceeded to pull out a small note-pad. I think Mr. Cook had instructed her to hold it low enough so it could not be seen, but that did not happen. Mr. Cook had obviously coached Jean on the questions he was going to ask, but as usual, Jean had to write everything down so she could try to remember. Just like her constantly obsessing about her day timer when living with us. Mr. Cook asked Jean his first question: How old are you? To which Jean replied, "Fifty." She is seventy-five. After some calendar work by Mr. Cook back and forth with Jean, she came to the conclusion she was seventy-five. This alone told me she was no better than she was when living with us eight months earlier.

Mr. Cook asked her another question and she immediately looked to the notepad. Matt was busy writing some notes and did not notice what was happening. I was sitting right behind Matt, so I started clearing my throat in hopes to get his attention. Terrie saw what was happening and nudged Matt to bring his attention to the notepad. Matt objected quickly, and the judge peered over the rail to see the notepad. The judge asked Jean to put the pad away. Jean said that she just wanted to make sure she answered the questions right. Of course, answering them right meant for her to be able to answer Mr. Cook's questions just as she had been coached to.

The judge explained that he understood, but it was not allowed in court. It was so obvious Mr. Cook had totally coached Jean on how he wanted her to answer his questions. After that, Jean was flustered. She could not answer the questions that Mr. Cook and Matt would go on to ask. It was also apparent that the judge was not happy with Mr. Cook's shenanigans in his courtroom. Still, Mr. Cook changed his tactics and tried to present Jean as "just fine" mentally, and that Terrie was just out to steal her money. I was thinking how ridiculous this was after everyone heard the doctor's testimony about lower one percentile of cognitive function, and an IQ of a seven-year-old child. I was also thinking, *This is going well, and Mr. Cook is sinking his own ship by defending Billy.*

The judge broke in and said that the hearing was only scheduled for three hours and that we were now six hours into it. He did not seem pleased. Mr. Cook indicated that he still had several other witnesses, so the judge scheduled an extension to reconvene in three weeks. So close, and now more waiting and wondering.

When court was adjourned and Jean left the courtroom, all of those other strangers who had been in the lobby swarmed Jean, telling her what a great job she had done on the stand, even though they didn't hear anything and did not know she couldn't answer the questions once her notepad had been disallowed. They were the vultures in wait, fawning over her with their big smiles and gleeful cheers for her.

When the day to continue was upon us, we were feeling hopeful. But we were not sure of anything at this point due to how much failure had happened to even get us to this juncture.

In the courtroom, everybody except Billy was allowed in, as there were no more witnesses after him. Interesting how the vultures were not there today. Everyone took their places and the judge entered.

Matt had just started his cross examination of Jean on the earlier date, so he continued with that process. Jean was so confused about everything. She could not explain what a trust was; she knew she had a trust and stated that nobody else was named in the trust even though Terrie was named as the co-trustee. She was asked about the changes to her professional team and her financial accounts, but could not answer correctly to any of them. I felt so bad for her, not knowing what had happened and how Billy had directed the entire thing. Jean kept correcting herself when she would say "we," to "I," so as not to implicate Billy as being with her at every turn, every telephone call, every meeting, everything—just as she was coached to do by Mr. Cook. But it was so telling each time she did this. It was an excruciatingly sad testimony, but one that gave us hope that we might yet have a conservator to watch over Jean.

Next on the stand was the Realtor who had sold Jean's house. She went on at length about how perky Jean was and how she was making all of the decisions about the sale of the home. When Matt was on cross with her, the Realtor could not explain why she had not found out that the house was in the family trust. He really grilled her on this, which created a great deal of doubt as to her credibility.

Then the new financial planner, who had assisted Billy in changing all of Jean's investments so Billy was beneficiary, took the stand. He, too, went on about how energetic Jean was. He even stated that he had had a twenty-five-year-old woman in his office right before Jean and Billy came in. He said that he thought Jean was every bit as on the ball as the younger client. On cross examination, Matt was able to really pin him down about making such drastic changes to Jean's portfolio. Items such as: "Didn't it seem suspicious that all of the changes were changed to benefit Billy and remove her daughter as beneficiary?" "Didn't it occur to you to contact her previous financial planner to find out more details before proceeding?" "Didn't it occur to you that these funds may be part of a trust or some other protection mechanism?" Of course, the agent said that he did not see any reason to do this because Jean seemed so "with it."

Next up was Billy. In short, Billy confessed that he was the one who called the police, and he was the one who called Elder Protective Services. When asked what proof he had about Terrie stealing money, he said that there was $12,000 missing from Jean's account. The $12K he brought up was the same thing Jean had brought up with Sherrie when they were going over the financials with Jean prior to all of this. It was a check Terrie had written to the IRS for the previous year's tax bill. When Billy was asked why he didn't just call Terrie to clear that up, he just shrugged. The judge made him answer for the record and he said, "I don't know." When asked about why he stated to Elder Protective Services that Terrie was stealing $20,000 per month from Jean, he just shrugged again, and had to answer aloud again, "I don't know." But there he was; he admitted to calling the police and lying, he admitted to calling Elder Protective Services and lying, he admitted lying to the judge about the restraining order. He was exposed for all to see, but still did not show any remorse whatsoever.

Mr. Cook then went down a line of questioning with Billy that was orchestrated to make Billy look like this elderly, kind, and caring man who was just concerned for Jean's well-being, and just how mean Terrie was toward him by never keeping him in the loop, which was an out-and-out lie. Billy was excused from the stand, but left the room instead of staying now that he had testified.

I was perplexed at how Mr. Cook was representing Jean, but he was covering for Billy even after his confession that he was the culprit stealing Jean away and taking control of all of her money. I wasn't the only one who recognized this action. Even the court stenographer would look our way with an expression of surprise during Billy's testimony.

Matt was first to give closing arguments. He did an extremely good job of reviewing the facts which had been presented. He went through the doctors' findings again, the facts of Billy's admissions of being the culprit, the facts of Billy changing Jean's financials, and the facts that Terrie had done what caring family members do in times of crises like these.

Then it was Mr. Cook's turn to make his closing statements. I could not believe my ears as he went on and on claiming that Billy was such a nice guy trying to help Jean, and how Billy was a victim in this matter. But when he neared the end of his statement, he went into this elaborate analogy of how a bee is physically not supposed to be able to fly, and yet the bee flies in spite of that. He then drew an analogy to Jean's situation, in which, he claimed, Jean was by all accounts not able to handle her own affairs, but that like the bee, the court should give her a chance to fly. Oh my God, did he just say that?! It seemed that Mr. Cook was off his rocker for his closing statement. It was ludicrous, but very helpful to our argument.

When Mr. Cook was finished with his closing statement, I don't think his butt had even hit the chair when the judge rendered his verdict. Matt had originally petitioned for Cognitive Impairment and Executive Function Disorder, and the judge found in favor for those two, but also added Subject to Undue Influence. He also approved Jess to be the conservator of record, then banged his gavel and left the courtroom. Just like that it was over, and people started to file out of the courtroom. Terrie and I were stunned; we had prevailed and the judge had thrown in an additional judgment of subject to undue influence. Terrie stood to face me over the rail; I grabbed her and we just held each other and cried.

On the way home, Terrie made calls to a few family members to tell them of the verdict. We stopped by the cemetery where her father and brother are buried. We just held each other for the longest time, still not believing that this nightmare had just taken a turn for the better, yet still knowing Jean would never be the same or a part of her real family ever again. A sense of relief washed over us and we reveled in how fighting the fight is the hardest choice, but sometimes worth the battle, especially for family. We had no idea of the turn of events about to happen.

So, you would think that having a court judge appoint a conservator to gain control of, and look after, Jean's finances would be a cut-and-dried scenario, right? Nope! Remember, applying common sense to the justice system is futile. You see, Billy was not in agreement with that decision. Jess was able to gain control of some of the finances that were in outside funds (i.e. PERS, Social Security, royalties), but the accounts which Billy still had his name on were being kept from her. For instance, Jess needed to get to the main checking account to set it up for automatic bill pay, but at first Billy dug his heels in to delay getting her that information. When Jess went to the bank to pull the appointed conservator card, Billy went in and changed the address related to the account. Because Jess did not have that address, the bank would not let her do anything with it. In addition, Mr. Cook was not being cooperative.

There was also the personal property of Jean's that had been moved to a storage locker. Billy would not cooperate with Jess to get an inventory of those assets. Jess had asked Jean to get her that inventory, but of course Jean is not able to do that due to her disability, and Billy would not help her.

In addition to these things was the fact that Jess could not get Jean to submit a budget for things she/they needed cash for. Once again, Billy would need to help Jean with it, but he refused to do so. Instead, Jess just calculated what their bills were and started to pay half of those, fully expecting Billy to pay his half. This is where things stood for a month or so, until Mr. Cook started harping on Jess to buy Jean a car to replace the one she lost in the wreck. Of course, Jean can no longer drive, but she is entitled to replace her car. We talked with Matt about this because it did not make sense, but Matt agreed that buying a car, even if Billy is the one driving it, was not something to be overlooked—if only for the sake of not giving Billy and Mr. Cook something to gripe about and allow them to, generally, stir the pot.

Jess was getting more and more frustrated with the situation and finally filed a petition to the court to have Billy removed from all accounts and to have the trust restored to what it was before the wreck, and to have the conservator exercise protected person's right to amend the trust.

Of course, another hearing would be months away, but at least Jess, and her attorney, were taking action. It's just very troublesome that any conservator would be required to take action regarding the same case after being granted the right to clean up this mess.

While waiting for the next hearing, we had conversations with Matt about what possible scenarios might be at hand until the hearing came up. One item that came up again was Jean's death. To be more precise, would Billy somehow perpetrate Jean's demise in order to get what monies he could now that his plan had been foiled? He has demonstrated that he will lie to police, lie to court judges, and continue to brainwash Jean into believing him completely . . . would he make the ultimate bad decision in order to get the money? Unfortunately, there is little any of us can do to prevent this, except pray. It is hard to fathom that we were doing everything we could to help keep her alive after the wreck and now we are discussing how Billy may play his final card, and there is nothing we can do directly to stop him.

Why?

The question of scientists, philosophers, students of anything, lovers and dreamers, forward-looking people . . . and those like us, trying to figure out how, in the grand scheme of things, we were selected to endure such heartache. Millions of people asking every day why deadly disease, sudden death, mental illness, war, old age, and any other malady that can afflict our loved ones, have to happen. There must be a wide variety of speculation, but no one knows for sure. Luck of the draw perhaps? Lessons still to be learned? An opportunity for personal growth, or a death spiral into guilt and self-doubt? To dwell on this question for any length of time is a practice in self-torture. No one knows for sure . . . why.

Could I have done something to avoid this? This question in introspective and honest reflection can wrack people with guilt because of poor decisions made, or free us from looking back because of the good decisions which were made.

Since the hearing, Terrie and I have had the mental freedom to review the path we have been on, and to ask ourselves this important question. Upon reflection, there were several times in which critical decisions needed to be made. Decisions we took time to evaluate with the information we had at hand at the time. Starting at the beginning, could we have done something about Billy? I suppose we could have been first to report to Elder Protective Services, but what would have been the result? Most likely, Billy would have been admonished for his interference in Jean's rehabilitation, but given Jean's state of mind, that move would have torn her apart even more. However, given the chance to report to Protective Services first, we would have made that move to protect Jean. She had already been unduly influenced by Billy, with the understanding that we were the enemy to her, and she most likely would have viewed this as the end of her world. She had talked of suicide, so would this have been the decision that pushed her over the edge? There is no clear answer to that.

What about when Officer Powers came into play?

Terrie and I discussed this at length when the officer had made her assumption quite clear that she believed Terrie had stolen money from Jean. Our conclusion was that no matter what we did, either hand over the financials or not, there was a good chance she was going to take it upon herself to knowingly or unknowingly give Billy the time to execute his plan. If we had handed over the financials to Officer Powers, she would have had the chance to make sure she was right, rather than answer to her superiors about how she could have made such egregious assumptions without proof. From our experience, we have observed that there are those in a position of power who can start to believe that power gives them the right to be above all whom they are charged to serve. Our thought was that there was such a person in front of us, talking wildly in face of the facts, not listening to our side of the story that Billy was the culprit, and not even willing to check that out because she felt her instincts were right and we were wrong, according to her. In the end, our decision to get a great lawyer and fight the fight is a decision we can live with. We did file a complaint to the police oversight people who look at complaints and then decide if they have merit enough to bring forward. This was early on, before the hearings. We had made a list of Officer Powers' actions we felt were completely out of line, but the reply we received back just took a few of those points and said that those particular points did not show she was in the wrong. They said that we could submit in writing to have the complaint forwarded to her supervisor, but here again was a situation where the oversight group was choosing to overlook some of what we had submitted. As before, we did not want to give them another chance to change the story before the story had been told in court.

Then there was the decision to allow Jean to be in continued isolation in order to have the restraining order rescinded. Of course, this was very tough as well. After several conversations with Matt about this, we decided to allow this because Terrie was not guilty and it would create a further delay to taking the legal actions needed to hopefully put a conservator in place. Not doing this would also allow Billy more time to dismantle Jean's estate, and then possibly divorce her to leave her high and dry financially.

Finally, the decision not to have Jess annul the marriage. Jess had brought it up and on the outside it looked like a good plan of action. But after discussing this move at length with Jess, Matt, and Jess's attorney, we decided not to have her pursue this course of action. The reasoning was twofold. First of all, it seems judges are very, very reluctant to do this and set that type of precedence. Secondly, because Jean was now totally brainwashed by Billy and Mr. Cook that everyone was against Billy, her new reality was that she wanted Billy more than anything. In her mind, Billy was her hero and she was happy to have been saved by him. In effect, she is happy where she is. So the same thinking as applied previously regarding going to Elder Protective Services first, applied here as well. To break them up would shatter Jean's new world. She would hate everyone involved and most likely fall into a state of despair. In addition, where would she go to live?

Certainly living with us would not be a possibility if she hated us.

Having her live in a facility would certainly not be her choice, but there were not any other viable options. We have always wanted her to be happy, so is it up to us to interfere with her new sense of happiness just because Billy is a bad man? The damage had been done, and the risk of worse things happening to Jean outweighed our desires. From the start, even before the wreck, we wanted her to have the financial means to live out her life in comfort. Having the conservator handling her financial affairs was the best chance Jean had of achieving that goal. Even though "comfort" meant living under Billy's rules in a dreary, makeshift, illegal living space in a pole barn. A painful decision, but one we carefully deliberated, understood, and could live with, barely.

The next hearing was upon us. We were feeling hopeful yet guarded; nothing seems cut and dried, although having the conservator's attorney now going before the judge with this petition, felt like we were more in the driver's seat. Of course, with Mr. Cook at the helm of defending Jean, anything was possible. We were fortunate to have the same judge preside over this hearing as well. Apparently, judges get together to see what's coming up and can take on cases that they have presided over before. A breath of common sense fresh air!

Dr. Hearst was up first just to reiterate his testimony from the first hearing. Mr. Cook tried to challenge him that Jean is all better now, but the doctor was having none of that.

Jean's brother, Dave, was called to testify from his home in Texas, to review the time right after Billy made his move and called Dave to tell him that Terrie was stealing money. Dave told the court that he told Billy he did not believe him and that he knew Terrie would never do such a thing. He also said Billy had never contacted him before that day, and that he told Billy to never contact him again.

Billy took the stand again, but played dumb. Over and over, claiming he didn't remember things he had said or done. The conservator's attorney did a good job of showing Billy testimony records and signatures from Elder Protective Services and police reports to jog his memory that he, alone, acted in this. Of course, there was Mr. Cook claiming what a great guy Billy is and that he never took Jean's money and it was all Terrie's fault just because she did not like Billy, and she only wanted all of the money for herself. On cross examination, the conservator's attorney did a great job of showing that Billy had not taken any money because Terrie had taken swift action to get the courts to stop him.

While Jess was on the stand, she explained in detail how Billy was not cooperating with her to get everything sorted out. She also dropped a couple of bombshells. The first was her recounting a meeting with Jean and Billy, where Billy exclaimed to Jean in the middle of the meeting that Terrie was stealing her money. Keep in mind we are nearly a year out from the first hearing, where Terrie was cleared of any wrongdoing. But Billy was still perpetuating the lie to Jean. Later in that meeting, Billy told Jean that Jess was not going to give them the money from the sale of Jean's house, then he got up and told Jean the meeting was over.

Terrie's parents had bought a piece of property in the central part of the state back in the 1970s. Her dad was so proud to have gotten in on the first parcels available. They put a tent trailer there and we would go there quite often to get away from the city. As time passed, Terrie's dad swapped out his parcels for two parcels which had become available, with the back border of the property up against BLM land with a great view of the mountains. Several years after that, he sold one of the parcels and netted enough cash to build a modular home there. He was just ecstatic about this, and it was called "The Ranch" thereafter. Terrie and I would go to the ranch often; it was so peaceful there and the lodge had a restaurant and a golf course we would play whenever we would go. It was a place for family, built by family, and enjoyed by our family for decades.

Once Billy had control of Jean, they started going there. We went once after that, but could tell Billy had been there. The place was filthy and didn't look like they had cleaned it for quite some time, which was odd for Jean as she and Terrie's dad were clean freaks. We had not been back since that time because it just felt dirty, both literally and figuratively. Knowing that he had slept there, and was with Jean there was more than unsettling to us, so we just stayed away.

Fortunately, Terrie's dad had the foresight to include the ranch in the family Trust. Once Jess had started having Terrie put certain items back into the Trust, in the name of the Trust, the ranch was one of those items. We had not been there for a couple of years, but we talked about what should be done. We wanted to go clean it up, but knew that Jean was still free to go there, which we liked, but we knew Billy would be the person accompanying her there. Terrie was just glad that it was back in the Trust, so we just left it at that, and didn't go there at that time for the same reasons we had stopped going altogether.

Terrie received a call from the owners association president. He said that they had an issue at the ranch property and the police had been called. Apparently Billy had threatened one of the neighbors while there and the neighbors had called the police. We decided that we needed to go there to check out the facts and talk with the neighbors about the situation. When we arrived, the ranch was intact, although from the outside it looked unkempt. When we tried to unlock the door we found that the lock had been changed. "What's his is his, and what's hers is his." Apparently Billy will stop at nothing to take everything from this family, but he had overstayed his welcome here with at least one neighbor, and we would get to the bottom of what he had done.

We had a locksmith come to the property and break in by picking the lock, and then had him install new door handles and a new deadbolt. When we entered the house, it was so filthy; cobwebs were strung between the furniture and tables, it had not been vacuumed for who knows how long, and the whole house stank. When I went out to check what was in the shed I found that they had not taken their garbage out with them for what looked like ever. Residents in the area could sign up for garbage service, but weekenders had to haul out their own garbage as they used their places. In the shed were eight giant bags full of household garbage.

Apparently, living in squalor was how Billy lived his life, and evidently Jean was now living this way as well, or didn't have a choice in the matter. We called the main office and explained the situation, and they kindly offered to let us take the garbage down and put it in one of their Dumpsters. I checked around the rest of the property and found that Billy had disposed of additional garbage and assorted old wood scraps by throwing everything over the fence onto the BLM property. I picked all of that up and disposed of it properly as well.

Terrie and I talked about the fact that the ranch was still open to Jean and ourselves, but how do we impart the need to keep it clean and not to touch or remove any family items acquired over decades of family use to a man (and I use the term loosely) we have had to take to court twice because he has attempted to steal all of Jean's money? Now it seemed he was going to try to lock us out of our own vacation home! We still needed to contact the neighbors to find out what exactly had happened, so perhaps Billy would solve this problem for us.

The neighbors had bought the house next door sometime while we had not been visiting the ranch. Terrie called the telephone number given to her by the association president to set up a time to talk. We met with the neighbors later that afternoon after they were home from their respective jobs. They are a young couple with three adorable little girls. The wife, Judy, worked at the golf course in the summer months and then at the club's restaurant in the winter. Her husband, Mike, worked in the nearby town. They are a great couple about the age of our son, and very happy to have been able to buy the house there and start a long, happy life together. Terrie immediately apologized for whatever had happened, and explained what we had been going through for the past years regarding Jean and Billy. The couple was so relieved to find out an explanation as to what had been happening and were excited that we were there to take charge of the situation.

So, what had happened? Judy explained that they had had a dispute with Billy over the eastern property boundary when they had first bought the property, and that Billy was uncooperative when they wanted to put a perimeter fence around their property. Rather than keep going around with Billy, they ended up putting their fence up about three feet short of the real property line so they would not have to disturb the trees which were on the property line, which was why Billy was throwing a fit, as they explained it. We asked what Jean's involvement was with this property dispute and if she was in the conversation. Mike explained that Jean had tried to get Billy to come in the house and quit arguing at one time, but Billy had just yelled at Jean to "get back in the house and shut up." Hmmmm. We had expected that Billy was probably overbearing to Jean, but now we are hearing of abusive behavior . . . heartbreaking, but not surprising.

As for the incident in question, Judy said that she and her girls were playing in their yard one day and she noticed a reflection coming from inside the ranch. She kept an eye on that reflection and had come to the conclusion that someone in our house was watching her and her girls with binoculars. Now Judy is one of those women who is about five feet nothin' and a hundred and nothin' pounds, but has the spunk of a pit bull, especially if you are doing anything to her family. So, Judy went over to the ranch house and confronted Billy about looking at them through binoculars.

Billy's response to Judy was, "That was not a pair of binoculars, that's the scope on my thirty-ought-six." Well isn't that right friendly?! Judy returned to her house and called the police. She filed a report with them and they came out to take her statement. The police said there was nothing they could do because she did not see a gun, so they told her to stay away from him and to call should he do or say anything to them again. Judy then called the homeowners association and filed a complaint there as well, which led to them calling Terrie. Of course, Terrie apologized profusely to Judy and Mike for what they had gone through, assured them this was unacceptable, and that they did the right thing by calling the police. Terrie also inquired if they had seen any other abusive behavior from Billy toward Jean. Mike stated that one day Billy was going to mow down the tall dry grass on the property with a tractor. Billy was driving and had Jean picking up rocks where he was going to mow. Mike said that Billy would keep yelling from the tractor, "Come on Jean, and pick up those rocks." This was hard to hear. Here was a seventy-seven-year-old woman with severe arthritis and a disabling head injury out picking up rocks while Billy cursed her.

Terrie called the officer who had taken the report from Judy and explained what had been happening with Billy. In the end, Terrie officially trespassed Billy from the property. That meant that if anyone called the police to report he was on the property, the police would come to arrest him. Of course, the police are concerned whenever there is a purported gun involved, and they had found that Billy has a concealed weapons permit, so if they were to come back, it would be a tense situation. Terrie explained to Judy and Mike what had transpired with the call to the police and asked them to call the police immediately should they see Billy there again. Judy and Mike were so relieved that we were there to try and take care of this, and happy that they actually had nice neighbors in charge and not Billy.

Terrie called an alarm company and had them come out and install a security system. I went into town and bought some cable and a lock to put across the driveway entrance. Terrie wrote an official trespass notice, as well as a letter to Jean to explain what had happened and that Billy was no longer allowed to be on the ranch property. Terrie also said in her letter to Jean that if she wanted to visit the property she was welcome to do so, and just needed to call Terrie to arrange for Terrie to take her there. She mailed both of those letters certified with copies sent to Matt and the police. Of course, days later, when we received the return receipts for the certified letters, Billy had signed for both of them, so there was no telling if Jean ever saw her letter, but most likely she did not.

On the evening of our anniversary we went into the nearby town about thirty minutes away for dinner at our favorite Italian restaurant there. It was good to be done with the cleanup and all of the other things that day at the ranch, so it was nice to just be a happily married couple again having an impromptu anniversary dinner. We had ordered our food and were sipping on cocktails when Terrie's phone rang.

It was Judy saying that Billy and Jean were at the ranch, and it looked like Billy was trying to get into the house. When it rains, it pours! Terrie asked that Judy not go over there, but just keep an eye on the house and that we would be there in about a half hour. We had our food boxed up and left hurriedly back to the ranch. As we were driving back, Mike called Terrie and said that Billy was unable to get into the house so they had left, but that Judy was following them in her car! Terrie asked Mike to call her off, but Mike said that once she got like this, there was no stopping her. Terrie called Judy's telephone and asked her to stop following them. Judy agreed and told Terrie which direction they were headed. This is a very rural area and there is only one highway through the area. I told Terrie that I would feel better knowing where they were and that they would not be making a surprise visit to the ranch in the middle of the night. We discussed it and decided that they could either drive to the next town and get a hotel room there, or head back to the big city that night. Either way, I wanted to know where they were for our own safety. As we were driving to the next town in the direction that Judy had said they were headed, I had to laugh that here we had just spent all that time at the ranch that day cleaning up that mess and securing the property and they show up that same day; what are the odds?!

When we arrived at the next town, we drove around the local hotels to see if they were staying there. I spotted Billy's car in the parking lot of a KFC, so we parked across the highway from there to see what they were going to do after they had their meal. I certainly did not want to confront Billy at this time because I was really worked up and did not want to be the one to escalate anything with him before he was officially notified of the trespass.

We waited a short time and Billy came out of the restaurant and walked across the parking lot to his car. Jean emerged a few seconds later with a bag of food and walked slowly and slightly hunched over to his car as well. Of course, Billy was already in the car, so opening the door for her was not going to happen, as if that would happen at any time anyway. They pulled onto the highway and headed back toward the city. That was a great relief to us, rather than have them still in the area that night. We have had enough sleepless nights over the past couple of years due to Billy. On the way back to the ranch, Terrie called Judy and Mike, as well as the police, to tell them what the situation was and that it appeared to be alright for now. Happy anniversary to us!

Of course, a few days later, Mr. Cook was on the phone with Matt regarding the trespass. Matt said he was quite upset and said that Mr. Cook was saying that Terrie and the crazy lady at the ranch were just making it all up to keep Billy away from the ranch. Matt explained that he was way off base and that it was clear that Mr. Cook had a real dual-representation issue by continually representing Billy, and that this was a very serious situation involving a gun. Mr. Cook discontinued the call quickly after that.

Billy had overplayed his cards this time and, once again, swift and decisive legal action on our part made sure that he would pay for his actions. The big upside is that he can no longer come to the ranch.

CHAPTER 20

Balancing Act

Jess has become so angry at Billy and Mr. Cook.

She called Matt to let him know that she and her attorney had decided to file a petition against Mr. Cook to have him removed as Jean's attorney. We agreed that something needed to be done, and although it would mean spending more trust money to do this, Mr. Cook was still protecting Billy at every turn even though he said he would stop representing Billy when Jess had confronted him after the last hearing. Of course, it would be months until that hearing came along. Not surprisingly, Mr. Cook turned around and filed a petition to have Jess removed as conservator because he felt she was unorganized and was not allowing Jean the money she needed.

Our take was that this was another easy way for Mr. Cook to rake in some more cash for himself at Jean's expense. Apparently, that's just one of the ways some attorneys play their get-rich game with the elderly. We also found out that Mr. Cook had filed for an appeal of the last ruling by the court, for Billy to turn in everything and be taken off of all the accounts. Well now, isn't that representing Billy again? This is getting out of hand, but an appeal can take years to get to court and Terrie was not concerned about that since the judge had conducted things properly and an appeal is based solely on procedure.

I think that reflection adds balance to our lives, if we are being fair and honest. Certainly we have run into quite a few people along this particular episode in our lives who have greatly disappointed us in the non-performance of their duties, and I don't think anyone would begrudge us if we were to be a little callous about those people. But in general, we are not going to lump entire groups of people into our emotions. We need police officers in order to protect us from bad people, and as a whole I respect the police for what they do.

The same would go for any first responder. They are the people who have taken up a cause to help people and that in itself is admirable. We personally know police and firefighters and can't say enough about the dangerous line of work they perform in and how appreciative we are for them. We all have got to find peace in our hearts and spread that peace around if we as a people are going to evolve past such behavior as we have seen.

The balance of mind and spirit is crucial, and we need to do our part to make neighborhood, city, country, planet, a better place to live. It is so very unfortunate that Terrie and I have had to endure a crisis like this, but we remain hopeful that by writing this book, it will be helpful to others who may find themselves in a similar situation, or who are going through something horrible right now. But in the end, we must be aware that there are those who may want to tear us down, and the only way to beat a bully is to stand up to the bully and use our words and the laws we agree to abide by, not hate.

I am sure there are those who read this book and say, "You need to sue everybody to expose them and teach them a lesson." But is it really our responsibility to do that? Terrie and I have discussed this many times and even though we feel people need to be held accountable, why should we spend all of our money suing Officer Powers, the restraining order judge, the caretaker company? Where do you even start with all that has happened? Besides, all the money in the world won't bring Jean back into our lives, and we feel so beat up mentally through the hearings and terror Billy has caused us, we need to find a better way. Perhaps a crack investigative reporter would like to uncover and expose the wrongdoings here and make public those who have perpetrated and trespassed upon us? We feel that helping regular people like ourselves to learn and prepare is the right thing to do for us. After all, suing the few people here in our town does not stop others in all of the other cities from being bad. If we can help people be better prepared through this story and by performing workshops and motivational talks, we are in effect actually helping society.

We have worked in corporate America and know that these organizations have dispute procedures for the public to follow, which are overseen by their attorneys. If we were to go down those paths, they would bring in their attorneys, and we would put ourselves in the position of waiting for more court procedures, having to deal with more stress, and most likely endure more bad people trying to cover their own backsides in the face of hard evidence.

Now this is not to say that we will not take legal action eventually, but at this time we are choosing to pick our battles carefully and not bite off more than we can chew. This issue is not over for us, so why create more battle lines and spend our money on fighting other fights? None of that will bring Jean back into the family. We feel it is a better use of our time to write this book and help all people understand what can happen and how you might elect to deal with each individual person and/ or circumstance. Nobody would learn anything by us taking on several legal battles.

We want to arm all of you with information and tools that you can draw upon now, or in the future. Only we as "The People" can fight the good fight by helping each other to understand things like the justice system rules or how some attorneys can be, how to recognize you have a wacky police officer standing in front of you, how to form good decision-making processes, how to keep emotions out of your decision-making processes, the critical need to put your affairs in order, and anything else you have been able to glean through these pages.

As a wise man once said, "Give a person a fish and they will eat for a day, teach a man to fish and he will eat forever." We want you to eat forever, even if there may be a time in your life that you will be involved with a death or injury in your family that may present problematic issues. Plan for it now while you have time! If you have not planned for it, you will be either helpless to do anything, or may spend every dime you have paying attorneys and the courts to get you out of a mess you may have been able to prevent if there had been a plan in place. It is not an attorney's job to advise you when you don't ask for advisement, it is their job to get you out of the mess you may be in. When was the last time your attorney called and asked if you have your affairs in order?

We want to start a movement to help people do just that—put their affairs in order. It's relatively easy when you know how, and most of the process can be done on your own, saving time and money. Putting your affairs in order is the single most proactive life decision you can make to preserve the well-being of everything you have worked so hard for all of your life. It's also one of the best financial decisions you could make to manage your wealth and protect your family.

Looking back, no one could have predicted our situation. So

remember, no one can predict yours either. However, if your affairs are in order you can be certain you're protected, no matter what happens to you or the ones you love. What if a parent meets a predator? What if they get dementia or suffer a brain injury? Looking back, we hadn't considered these things—but, because we were prepared legally, we gave Matt the legal high ground to fight for Jean.

When a loved one is isolated, it's like watching a fish surrounded by a school of sharks, from the back of the boat. There's not much you can do but watch, as the fish gets devoured helplessly. While we did not stand by and watch Jean get devoured, it still seemed as if the sharks circled endlessly. Every single decision she made seemed influenced by someone with devious intentions. It felt as if we were the only ones seeing clearly. Jean could not make decisions of any complexity at all.

Mr. Cook would always say, "This is what Jean wants," but there is no way on earth that Jean could even understand, let alone construct legal petitions. Due to the isolation created by Billy, and then carried forward by his attorney, Mr. Cook has always said in conversations, "This is what Jean wants."

From what I had been able to learn about cognitive function in this short time, and from my layman's point of view, it is the ability of the working memory to learn, deduce, comprehend, store, recover, and use information. I would describe it as multi-dimensional thinking. First, for example, one would need to remember what "time" is and how it applies to everyday life. Then, remember what a clock is and what its function is —what the hands are for and how they correlate with the numbers on the clock, and also try to remember how to draw using a pencil. The result of mentally juggling this information and then determining the correct time is the end result. Using the "draw a clock" example of testing, Jean would have to recall these different individual components in an exact manner in order to draw a clock.

With Jean, she knew she should know how to do this, but it was just not possible for her to think beyond one dimension at a time, let alone the eight components described above. If we asked Jean how she was feeling, she would say, "Well, I'm not sure." If we asked her if she felt better, she would say "yes." This is one-dimensional thinking (i.e., "better, yes.") But asking her what felt better, she would not be able to ascertain that information because it required her to deduce several things to arrive at a conclusion. She no longer had the ability to recall the information she needed to reconstruct the information needed to deduce and construct a conclusion to a question.

When our court date came, Jess's attorney appointed another attorney to present the case since Matt and Jess's attorney would be witnesses this time around, and as such would not be allowed to present. We had our usual court day breakfast and went over to the courthouse. It was being held in the same room and by the same judge as before, thank goodness.

We met with Jess's attorney and Matt in the lobby of the courtroom for some chitchat while we waited. A young man walked in and was introduced to us as Dick, the attorney presenting the case. He was a slight young man who was eagerly awaiting the start of the hearing. He seemed to be cocksure of himself as he thumbed through papers and chatted with the other attorneys. I said to Matt that Dick seemed to be a young go-getter. "Is he good?" Matt replied, "Well, we will see."

Billy was not there, most likely Mr. Cook's way of showing that he was not representing him. Mr. Cook was also going to represent himself in the case, which did not surprise anyone considering the ego he has displayed.

Dick called Matt to the stand and asked him questions regarding his involvement with Mr. Cook. Matt was quite clear of his reservations as to Mr. Cook's motives and that he felt he was definitely representing both Billy and Jean. He told of the many telephone conversations with Mr. Cook where he had told him that he is the only one who seemed to think Billy is a nice guy in the face of all of the evidence, and even in the face of Billy's testimonies.

Next up was Jess's attorney. He also told the court of Mr. Cook's actions regarding Billy, and how Mr. Cook had done nothing to help Jess or encourage Billy to cooperate. He also told of a telephone conversation where they were discussing the fact that Mr. Cook was not paid part of his requested compensation because he was clearly representing Billy. He said in that conversation that Mr. Cook said he would just have Jean gift Billy the money to pay him.

Now it was Mr. Cook's turn to call witnesses. He called up a man we had never met before who claimed to be a friend of Jean's from back in her school teaching days. This guy was never part of Terrie's parents' inner circle of friends. According to his testimony, he used to be a special needs teacher and was now involved in somehow helping Jean to get better. He was certainly excited to be helping Jean, but obviously had no knowledge of what had taken place previous to today. He was helping Jean, which was a good thing, at least someone was, but he was also just dug up by Mr. Cook to aide in his case.

Next up, he called another attorney who specialized in law ethics. This woman was very professional and defended Mr. Cook's case that he needed to keep representing Jean even though Billy was in the mix. She really did not talk toward the reason we were there, but more to the case that Jean needed Mr. Cook. I was dumbfounded that Dick did not bring this fact out on cross examination.

Next, Mr. Cook called up another psychologist who had apparently seen Jean with the intention of analyzing her current mental status. This doctor explained that he had gone through some of the testing but could quickly recognize that Jean had not improved more than what Dr. Hearst had discovered two years before. This doctor even said on the stand that his counsel, Mr. Cook, probably would not be pleased to hear that, but that was his conclusion.

Then, this doctor traveled down a whole different path of testimony. He said that he was amazed at how Jean showed good function in other parts of her brain that allowed her to still sing songs and perform other tasks related to long-term memory. Then Mr. Cook pulled one of his tricks again. He suddenly wanted to introduce new evidence that would prove Jean is just fine and able to take care of herself. Mr. Cook always has demonstrated a propensity to show that Jean is just fine, but now he was doing it in a hearing that was about dual representation.

He asked the court if he could present a video showing how well Jean performs when not under the pressure of the court. Dick was flustered at this move. I saw the deer-in-the-head-lights look, and in my mind was pleading for him to object to this part of the Mr. Cook three-ring circus act he has always done. But no, instead Dick allowed a video testimony of something not provided to him before the hearing, and he had no idea what was going to be shown on the video. Mr. Cook's assistant set up a laptop computer and they ran the video. This video is clearly at the doctor's office and Billy is there with Jean as well. The doctor leads Jean through a complement of prearranged questions which she has obviously been coached on and yet she becomes confused several times. The doctor keeps goading Jean until she starts to become emotional and then asks her if she wants to see her daughter again. Jean starts crying and says, if "they" (meaning us) won't accept Billy as her husband, then she does not want to see us ever again. For me, what was sad was the way that the doctor led Jean down the path and then into a preorchestrated statement like that. I was appalled by this, it was unscrupulous, and Jean was being treated no better than an animal in a circus. Even worse was that Dick just sat there, no objections, nothing! Even worse still, Dick barely cross examined the doctor at all.

This is the frustration of legal matters.

Suddenly, as I was bewildered by the events at hand, Dick stood up and said to the judge that he thought this was only scheduled for three hours and that he had another appointment scheduled at one o'clock that he can't miss.

What!?

Then Dick played right into Mr. Cook's hands. The judge asked Mr. Cook how long he needed to finish and his reply was, "Oh, 15 minutes should do it." The judge asked Dick if he could wait that long, to which he agreed. So, it is now 12:00 and Mr. Cook knows that Dick will have to be out of there by 12:30, so what does Mr. Cook do? He talks on for another 30 minutes, of course. So, now it's Dick's turn to give his closing argument and he says to the judge, "I'm turning into a pumpkin here, your honor." Dick then gives about a two-minute closing argument that holds no weight whatsoever and that was it, over.

The judge then said that it would take extraordinary circumstances to remove an attorney from a case, and he was not in a position to do that today, and "the court denies the petition as filed." Bang the gavel, that's that.

Young Dick quickly gathered his files and fled the courtroom to his next appointment.

Let me say one thing here that is crystal clear to us. The justice system is only as good as the attorney you have representing you.

CHAPTER 21

We Are Not Alone

We have learned that many others have also had family members who were excessively influenced by someone who came into their lives.

There are a variety of reasons why this can happen, not just because of a brain injury. A person might allow themselves to be overly influenced because they're lonely. There are millions of people who feel disconnected, as if they have no one to turn to, no one to count on. So to have someone come into their life, who appears to really care about them, can make them feel pretty special.

They may become so dependent on this individual that they will do things that are not normally in their nature simply to keep this person around and to keep from returning to that lonely place in their life. Who are the influencers? It could be the women he meets while bowling, that friendly looking guy at dance classes, the person in the coffee shop all seemingly innocent at arm's length. But they're all looking for someone, someone they can have control over. Those people who like to be in total control of everything around them. Those who see opportunity to gain something from another individual will also fall into the same category.

CHAPTER 22

More Surprises

Matt called us to inform us that Jess was resigning from the case. He said that she felt kicked in the gut regarding the loss of the hearing to have Mr. Cook removed, and she was so frustrated from having to deal with Mr. Cook and Billy.

Well, that was certainly a bombshell! Just quit, kicked in the gut, frustrated. We have no doubt that Jess feels this way, but just quit? So sorry our case is a tough one. Of course, the next hearing is the one filed by Mr. Cook to have Jess removed as conservator, so perhaps she wasn't ready to face that. After all, losing a hearing like that would tarnish one's reputation.

We met with Matt to talk about a replacement conservator. He suggested a couple of people who would be good, but of course Mr. Cook, I mean Jean, would have to agree to the choice. We chose based on the new conservator being a man who might be able to stand up to Mr. Cook's temperament, and also, the lawyer for this firm was supposed to be a fierce litigator in the courtroom. Surprisingly, Mr. Cook agreed to the choice, and off we went again.

We have now met with the new conservator, Mr. Carver a couple of times. He has a clear picture of what has transpired and is working to make sure that everything the court decided has been taken care of. One item that apparently Jess had not taken care of was the inventory of Jean's physical assets from her house after it was sold. Mr. Carver arranged for us to meet with one of his staff who is in charge of such things for their company.

We met at the storage site and he let us into the locker. Terrie's parents had once made a list of items which were to be kept in the family generationally, items which had been passed down from many generations. Many of these items had been brought over from Europe and then transported by wagon down through Canada and on to North Dakota. The sentimental and nostalgic value of these items is priceless. They give a sense of family, along with the stories that came along with them.

We knew by the size of the storage locker that not all of the household items were there; it was just too small. Terrie was just hoping against hope that the generational items were still there. When the locker was opened, it was apparent not all of them were there. Not only that, but where were all of the other furnishings? Four generations of furniture and other items just gone! Terrie felt violated again and she was understandably upset regarding this. As much as we tried to prepare for this worst outcome, it was still unbelievably tragic.

This situation is certainly not over for us. At some point, either Billy or Jean will pass away, and we will have to enter the legal fray once again in order to sort things out.

In addition, Mr. Cook has continued to try and insert himself. While writing this book, he contacted Matt to say he thought we should try and work out some global settlement to make this go away. Matt asked Mr. Cook what he was proposing. Mr. Cook stated that Jean wants to be able to go to the ranch again, and that she also wants the family Trust to take care of Billy should something happen to her. So, Mr. Cook is proposing that this global settlement is what Jean wants even though she cannot even think in these ways without being unduly influenced, and the things Mr. Cook claims Jean wants only benefit Billy. We would say "unbelievable," but nothing surprises us regarding Mr. Cook's ways.

Even as the new conservator is taking over the case and coming up to speed, Mr. Cook approached the conservator's attorney asking for the same global settlement with the exact same terms.

To us, this is so ridiculous. To agree to these terms would put the neighbors at the ranch in possible danger, and having the trust agree to take care of Billy would motivate him to make sure Jean will not survive him.

Matt sent the following email to the new conservator's attorney.

> *Rebecca,*
>
> *I had similar discussions with Mr. Cook in the past and found it quite difficult to put together distinct provisions of a global settlement. My client would certainly support such, but one of the sticky points will likely be the trust issues. My client's decision to exclude Billy from the property has been a real issue for the other side. Please note that Jean is welcome there anytime, just not with Billy. Mr. Cook also wanted more money flowing to the household, but Jess found that what money was given to Jean was not spent.*
>
> *Finally, there was some discussion in the past about all parties agreeing to a modification of an agreed upon estate plan, which was basically being discussed as, 'What's in this*

for Billy?' However, Mr. Cook was roughly speaking of a plan where Billy would have a lifetime interest in Jean's assets with the remainder interest continuing to the family as set up by the late husband and Jean. Quite frankly, with the previous transfers, changed beneficiary designations, the will being revoked by the marriage, and the potential of a spousal elective share, Billy will do quite well without any agreement.

This whole discussion is quite distasteful for my client as she sees Billy as victimizing her mother. My client does concede that Jean states her desire to be with Billy, however she believes this is borne from her mother's incapacity and Billy's undue influence (with the complicit involvement of Mr. Cook). There is no good answer here, but I think you will find that my client has acted reasonably throughout this tragic episode of her mother's life and will continue to do so.

While I may not be able to give you specific positions from my client at this point, and do not have any authority to bind her to an agreement, I will tell you that she will not likely voluntarily resign as Trustee without at least Mr. Cook's agreement to resign as Jean's counsel. I have spoken with Mr. Cook on this issue several times and he says it is a non-starter because Jean wants him as her attorney.

On the flip side I note that while she had capacity, Jean wanted my client to be her Trustee, so did her late husband. Even ignoring the mental capacity, conflict of interest, and undue influence issues, Mr. Cook refuses to acknowledge that he can unilaterally agree to stand down in the best interest of his client. However, my client does not believe Mr. Cook cares about Jean and believes that the real issue here is Mr. Cook's personal interest in continued large fee payments. Again, I cannot bind my client, but I would certainly have a long talk with her about continuing as Trustee if you could get an agreement where qualified and appropriate counsel was substituted for Mr. Cook. Let me know if you want me to discuss this in any more detail with my client. Otherwise I will wait to hear back from you before I discuss this matter with her. I thank you for contacting me on these issues.

Matt

CHAPTER 23

Dear Reader,

Are you prepared?

Hopefully after reading this book, you'll be better equipped to face the family challenges that you've read about. We hope something like this never happens to you. But if it has, please know you're not alone.

As we have moved through our ordeal, the amount of people who are not legally prepared to deal with a family catastrophe kept coming up and entered our conversations regularly. As we thought about our lives and our professional careers helping people make big life decisions, we felt an obligation to help more people put their affairs in order. We suppose it's our way of making lemonade out of the lemons we have been given.

"Putting your affairs in order" is a common term for many,

but also unfamiliar to others. Statistics on how many people have not done this ranges from 50 percent, to insurance industry estimates somewhere north of 60 percent. Even if we work with the low number of 50 percent, when you know what is at stake, it is an alarming number.

In 2013, Consumer Reports found that just over $1 billion dollars had not been claimed through life insurance companies. Much of this was because the person who died had not informed their heirs of the policy, and this is just one of hundreds of aspects needing attention when you need to step in, or someone is stepping in for you. So, how do you know what you don't know when it comes to all of the details of someone's life . . . especially when they are not there mentally or physically able to help? You don't. It has to happen before something happens, and there is no easy way around this fact.

As we looked more closely and talked with people, it was clear that the need to prepare crosses all ethnic, religious, and socioeconomic circles. Not only that, but as we moved into the information age the problems were compounded by the control mechanisms of the information we need access to for someone else; for example: user names and passwords.

As a result, in 2013 we started live presentations and workshops to demonstrate how easy it is to put your affairs in order. The fact is, it is not that expensive, either, if you know what to do. Eighty percent of the task can be done on your own, with the other 20 percent done by an estate attorney who will be able to put everything in the proper legal format which best suits your needs and family circumstances. Our presentations have been extremely well received and we have dedicated ourselves to empower as many people as possible to take control of this part of their legacy. Keep in mind, if something happens to you or a loved one and you have not put your affairs in order, it will be too late and there is nothing you can do at that point but take the long, time-consuming, expensive, and heartbreaking route. We have a website you can go to, www.ALegacyUndone.com, for information on how to schedule us for a presentation or find out when we will be in your town. We also have a Facebook page at www.facebook.com/ALegacyUndone where you can tell us your story and read how others have triumphed or coped, creating a place for conversation and community for those taking action.

There are so many benefits of putting your affairs in order.

The peace of mind in knowing that you are protecting your family is priceless. It is also one of the most important financial actions you will take to help make sure your affairs stay with whom you want them to. Powers of attorney, wills, and trusts protect you and your family in far reaching ways; take our story for example. Having our family trust in place gave our lawyer the legal teeth needed to prevent Billy from keeping what was left of Jean's money and estate. We all work very hard for most of our lives, and performing these simple tasks keeps your fortune in the family, not in the pockets of criminals and those who will be paid to unravel the mess you may find yourself in.

As we have seen, the "middle class" of America has been stripped to bare bones in some cases; putting your affairs in order may be the single best way to help future generations of your family to have a better foothold on their future. For example, let's say you set up in your trust for college funds to go to grandchildren. They in turn will have the opportunity to go to college, whereas, without those funds they may not be able to. Who knows whether they in turn might produce the next great idea or invention that helps save lives, or ends hunger in the world! Without that boost you created by being forward-looking and taking action, these things may never come to fruition. There are thousands of possibilities, and these steps to a better future may be the only way the middle class can make a comeback. Your commitment to putting your affairs in order, starting today, is a wise decision for you and your family, for generations to come.

Lastly, we all need to be talking to our children about this once they turn a reasonable age, and for those who have parents who have not indicated they have prepared, please speak with them and help them pull everything together in a kind and caring manner.

We are the teachers for our children—teach well and lead by example.

We wish you a long and happy life!

Terrie & Jon

ACKNOWLEDGMENTS

This book would never have been written in this way without the help of some incredibly giving professionals. Tammy Kling, our editor/ghost writer, shaper of stories, and encourager to just keep writing. Your wisdom and caring kept us writing through the tough stuff, so we could get to the teaching of the good stuff. Joanne McCall, you have inspired us, taught us, and brought the best out in us to take on the new journey at hand. Erin Donley, you came into our lives for totally unrelated reasons, and later, pointed us toward those mentioned above. Thank you, Larry Carpenter, at Clovercroft Publishing, for recognizing the relevance of our story. Thank you, NaKina Carr Talbert, your support and book title epiphany are so valuable to us.

To our son, who should never have been made to bear what he had to bear. We love you so much!

To family members and close friends who listened quietly while we told of the unthinkable. Thank you for listening.

To "Matt," for being a great lawyer, litigator, and a compassionate man when everything around us was falling apart.

To "Deanna," for helping us to see further into ourselves than we thought possible. Your compassion, wisdom, and professional techniques allowed us to keep fighting even when we felt broken.

To "Sherrie," thank you for supporting "Jean" all of those years and helping to fight this evil. You are important and loved.

To our personal Facebook family of friends. Even though only a very few were aware of our story, posting your thoughts, humor, and kindness kept us connected to the crazy, wonderful world outside of our personal saga. Just being you helped us more than we can ever express. Special thanks to Glynn Shannon for reminding Jon of tolerance, and Iris Harrison for test reading and helping us to bring more detail to the characters.

Last, but not least, to "Jean." We love you and miss you . . . wherever you are.